SELF-LEARNING MANAGEMENT SERIES

DATA STRUCTURES AND ALGORITHMS ESSENTIALS

YOU ALWAYS WANTED TO KNOW

Learn efficient coding and problem-solving in
Python, with code samples in Java, C++, and JavaScript

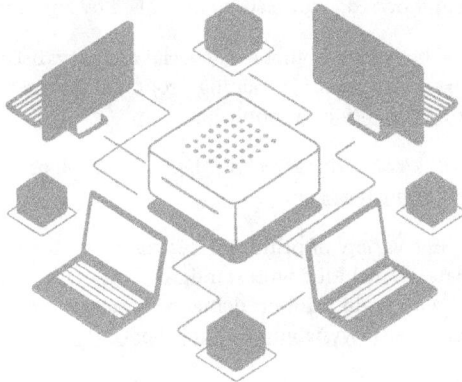

SHAWN PETERS

DATA STRUCTURES AND ALGORITHMS ESSENTIALS YOU ALWAYS WANTED TO KNOW

First Edition

Published by Vibrant Publishers LLC, USA, www.vibrantpublishers.com

Paperback ISBN 13: 978-1-63651-632-5
Ebook ISBN 13: 978-1-63651-633-2
Hardback ISBN 13: 978-1-63651-634-9

Library of Congress Control Number: 2025945478

This publication is designed to provide accurate and authoritative information regarding the subject matter covered. The Author has made every effort in the preparation of this book to ensure the accuracy of the information. However, information in this book is sold without warranty, either expressed or implied. The Author or the Publisher will not be liable for any damages caused or alleged to be caused either directly or indirectly by this book.

All trademarks and registered trademarks mentioned in this publication are the property of their respective owners, including but not limited to Python. These trademarks are used for editorial and educational purposes only, without intent to infringe upon any trademark rights. This publication is independent and has not been authorized, endorsed, or approved by any trademark owner.

Vibrant Publishers' books are available at special quantity discounts for sales promotions, or for use in corporate training programs. For more information, please write to bulkorders@vibrantpublishers.com

Please email feedback/corrections (technical, grammatical, or spelling) to spellerrors@vibrantpublishers.com

Vibrant publishes in a variety of print and electronic formats and by print-on-demand. Some material included with standard print versions of this book may not be included in e-books in print-on-demand. To access the complete catalog of Vibrant Publishers, visit www.vibrantpublishers.com

Exclusive Online Resources for You

As our valued reader, your purchase of this book includes access to exclusive online resources designed to enhance your learning experience. These resources can be downloaded from our website, www.vibrantpublishers.com, and are created to help you apply Data Structures and Algorithms concepts effectively.

Online resources for this book include the following:

1. **Case studies and real-world problems,** such as "Managing Customer Support Resources" and "Warehouse Organization and Efficient Product Placement"

2. **Chapter-aligned coding tasks** to help you practice and test your understanding as you learn

3. **Downloadable code samples** (in Python, Java, C++, and JavaScript) for all key code discussed in the book

Why these online resources are valuable:

- **Practical application:** The case studies connect theory to reality by showing how data structures and algorithms drive decisions in real business situations.

- **Step-by-step guidance:** The coding tasks walk you through applying each concept, reinforcing how and why specific structures and techniques are chosen.

- **Hands-on acceleration:** The downloadable code lets you experiment immediately, adapt working solutions, and build confidence across multiple languages.

How to access your online resources:

1. **Visit the website:** Go to www.vibrantpublishers.com
2. **Find your book:** Navigate to the book's product page via the "Shop" menu or by searching for the book title in the search bar.
3. **Request the resources:** Scroll down to the "Request Sample Book/Online Resource" section.
4. **Enter your details:** Enter your preferred email ID and select "Online Resource" as the resource type. Lastly, select "user type" and submit the request.
5. **Check your inbox:** The resources will be delivered directly to your email.

Alternatively, for quick access: simply scan the QR code below to go directly to the product page and request the online resources by filling in the required details.

Happy learning!

SELF-LEARNING MANAGEMENT SERIES

TITLE	PAPERBACK* ISBN

BUSINESS AND ENTREPRENEURSHIP

BUSINESS COMMUNICATION ESSENTIALS	9781636511634
BUSINESS ETHICS ESSENTIALS	9781636513324
BUSINESS LAW ESSENTIALS	9781636511702
BUSINESS PLAN ESSENTIALS	9781636511214
BUSINESS STRATEGY ESSENTIALS	9781949395778
ENTREPRENEURSHIP ESSENTIALS	9781636511603
INTERNATIONAL BUSINESS ESSENTIALS	9781636513294
PRINCIPLES OF MANAGEMENT ESSENTIALS	9781636511542

COMPUTER SCIENCE AND TECHNOLOGY

BLOCKCHAIN ESSENTIALS	9781636513003
CYBERSECURITY ESSENTIALS	9781636514888
MACHINE LEARNING ESSENTIALS	9781636513775
PYTHON ESSENTIALS	9781636512938

DATA SCIENCE FOR BUSINESS

BUSINESS ANALYTICS ESSENTIALS	9781636514154
BUSINESS INTELLIGENCE ESSENTIALS	9781636513362
DATA ANALYTICS ESSENTIALS	9781636511184

FINANCIAL LITERACY AND ECONOMICS

COST ACCOUNTING & MANAGEMENT ESSENTIALS	9781636511030
FINANCIAL ACCOUNTING ESSENTIALS	9781636510972
FINANCIAL MANAGEMENT ESSENTIALS	9781636511009
MACROECONOMICS ESSENTIALS	9781636511818
MICROECONOMICS ESSENTIALS	9781636511153
PERSONAL FINANCE ESSENTIALS	9781636511849
PRINCIPLES OF ECONOMICS ESSENTIALS	9781636512334

*Also available in Hardback & Ebook formats

SELF-LEARNING MANAGEMENT SERIES

TITLE	PAPERBACK* ISBN

HR, DIVERSITY, AND ORGANIZATIONAL SUCCESS

DIVERSITY, EQUITY, AND INCLUSION ESSENTIALS	9781636512976
DIVERSITY IN THE WORKPLACE ESSENTIALS	9781636511122
HR ANALYTICS ESSENTIALS	9781636510347
HUMAN RESOURCE MANAGEMENT ESSENTIALS	9781949395839
ORGANIZATIONAL BEHAVIOR ESSENTIALS	9781636512303
ORGANIZATIONAL DEVELOPMENT ESSENTIALS	9781636511481

LEADERSHIP AND PERSONAL DEVELOPMENT

DECISION MAKING ESSENTIALS	9781636510026
INCLUSIVE LEADERSHIP ESSENTIALS	9781636514765
INDIA'S ROAD TO TRANSFORMATION: WHY LEADERSHIP MATTERS	9781636512273
LEADERSHIP ESSENTIALS	9781636510316
TIME MANAGEMENT ESSENTIALS	9781636511665

MODERN MARKETING AND SALES

CONSUMER BEHAVIOR ESSENTIALS	9781636513263
DIGITAL MARKETING ESSENTIALS	9781949395747
MARKETING MANAGEMENT ESSENTIALS	9781636511788
MARKET RESEARCH ESSENTIALS	9781636513744
MODERN ADVERTISING ESSENTIALS	9781636514857
SALES MANAGEMENT ESSENTIALS	9781636510743
SERVICES MARKETING ESSENTIALS	9781636511733
SOCIAL MEDIA MARKETING ESSENTIALS	9781636512181

*Also available in Hardback & Ebook formats

SELF-LEARNING MANAGEMENT SERIES

TITLE	PAPERBACK* ISBN

OPERATIONS MANAGEMENT

AGILE ESSENTIALS	9781636510057
OPERATIONS & SUPPLY CHAIN MANAGEMENT ESSENTIALS	9781949395242
PRODUCT MANAGEMENT ESSENTIALS	9781636514796
PROJECT MANAGEMENT ESSENTIALS	9781636510712
STAKEHOLDER ENGAGEMENT ESSENTIALS	9781636511511

CURRENT AFFAIRS

DIGITAL SHOCK	9781636513805

*Also available in Hardback & Ebook formats

About the Author

Shawn Peters is an experienced educator with a passion for technology. He holds a Bachelor of Science degree with a major in Physics and a minor in Mathematics from Memorial University. He began his teaching career focusing on science and mathematics education, but in recent years has shifted his focus toward computer science, driven by his long-standing love of programming. He received certification in Python Programming Teaching from the College of the North Atlantic.

In addition to his 20 years as a junior and senior high school educator, Shawn also works in curriculum development and as a freelance programmer specializing in Python, JavaScript, and Java. His recent journey into programming was fueled by his lifelong passion for the subject. As a child, he began programming in GW-Basic and QBasic, and experimenting with HTML for simple website design, though he never pursued formal training at that time. Throughout his teaching career, Shawn found ways to incorporate programming into his teaching methods, and began exploring programming more comprehensively, gradually shifting from teaching science and mathematics to focusing more on technology courses.

Shawn enjoys creating artwork using JavaScript and the p5.js library, blending his background in mathematics and physics with a creative approach to coding. His work often explores systems-based design, using algorithms to generate visual art. He views algorithm design not only as a technical exercise but also as a form of creative expression. He also develops applications in Python, focusing on puzzles, intelligent signal processing, and interfacing with Raspberry Pi.

Shawn is the author of *Python Essentials You Always Wanted To Know*, a practical introduction to the basics of computer programming with Python, aimed at both learners and educators. He is currently developing a YouTube series focusing on the content of the book. Whether writing, creating, teaching, or coding, Peters is committed to making technology accessible, creative, and meaningful.

What Experts Say About This Book!

An excellent guide for learning the basics of data structures and algorithms with simple explanations and useful examples.
– Pintu Kumar, Research Scholar, IEOR, IIT Bombay

Packed with clear explanations of essential DSA concepts, this book is a must-have for anyone serious about mastering data structures and algorithms in Python.
– Karthik Chandrakant, AI Leader; Head of Data Science & AI at Imarticus Learning; Ex-Amazon, Mu Sigma; TEDx Speaker, Author

Data Structures and Algorithms Essentials You Always Wanted to Know provides a clear, structured, and beginner-friendly introduction to core data structures and algorithms using Python. Each chapter balances theory, practical applications, and quizzes that reinforce learning, making it ideal for self-learners and early computer science and data science students. The inclusion of real-world examples, such as caching and file systems, helps bridge the gap between abstract concepts and hands-on coding. Since I opened the book, I couldn't close it. If you want to learn data structures concepts, this is the learning material for you.
– Dr. Lawrence Decamora, Computer Science Instructor, University of Santo Thomas

The book delivers a strong educational experience characterized by clarity, accuracy, and pedagogical effectiveness. It excels at introducing foundational computer science concepts to beginners while maintaining practical relevance through real world coding examples.
– Aldo Baca, Senior Machine Learning Scientist

What Experts Say About This Book!

Shawn Peters' book does a great job of explaining how data structures and algorithms are used with real life examples, making complex ideas easy to grasp. I especially loved the way he uses pie baking as a fun illustration—it turns a tricky concept into something clear and relatable. The language is simple, avoiding jargon, and the illustrations really help make the ideas stick. It's inspiring to see how these skills can be applied in professional settings, linking everyday understanding to real-world problem-solving. Overall, it's an engaging and practical read that makes learning data structure and algorithms both accessible and relevant to everyday and professional life.

– Loo Yee NG, Solutions Architect, CTMG

Shawn Peters has created an excellent guide for anyone studying computer science or data science, whether at school, university, or learning independently. This book offers a comprehensive and accessible introduction to essential topics like data structures, arrays, Big O notation, stacks, queues, linked lists, hash tables, trees, graphs, and dynamic programming. With clear explanations, practical Python and pseudocode examples, and real-world applications, it's a valuable resource for learners preparing for exams, interviews, or building a strong foundation in coding. A smart, well-structured read for students and aspiring developers alike.

– Jonathan Gillespies, Computer Science & Business Teacher

Table of Contents

Preface

When I wrote *Python Essentials You Always Wanted To Know*, I wrote it for anyone who wanted to begin their programming journey but felt they had missed their chance. I wrote it for people who were intimidated by the rapid pace of change, who didn't see themselves represented in tech, or who had simply set programming aside to pursue other careers or paths. That book was about starting from where you are.

This book is about what comes next.

Over the past few years, I've had the opportunity to work more deeply with data structures, algorithms, and problem-solving--both in my teaching and in my personal practice. As a self-taught programmer, much of what I know has come from working on projects and filling in the gaps in my own knowledge as I gain experience. At one point, I stumbled into the world of online coding challenges. Eager to test my skills I jumped in and at first I felt like I was doing alright. But very quickly, I realized I knew far less than I thought I did. Instead of admitting defeat, I leaned in and embraced this new challenge.

As I've developed my programming skills, I've learned that a strong foundation in algorithm design can not only improve code but also change how you see problems. You begin to recognize patterns, reduce clutter, and build tools that are efficient, adaptable, and creative. Whether you're optimizing code, designing interactivity, processing data, or experimenting with generative systems, algorithmic thinking is what connects logic to creation.

That's the spirit of this book. It goes beyond definitions and syntax to focus on how algorithmic thinking can be used to solve real problems. If my first book was about overcoming hesitation, this one is about building confidence. Whether you're learning, teaching, or returning to code after time away, I hope this helps you take the next step, not just in understanding data structures and algorithms, but in putting them to work.

Introduction to the Book

This book is designed to help you move beyond the basics of Python programming. As you've begun your programming journey, you've likely encountered situations where your code doesn't scale well. There's nothing inherently wrong with the code itself, but with larger inputs, it begins to slow down. Now that you know how to write code, it's time for you to learn how to write efficient code, considering the time and space complexity of the algorithms you use.

This isn't a guide to learning new syntax or memorizing definitions; instead, it focuses on how problems can be structured, broken down, and solved using algorithmic techniques. With a basic understanding of Python, a sense of curiosity, and a willingness to tackle complex problems, this book will guide you through understanding and applying advanced data structures.

The chapters in this book build upon one another, starting with fundamental concepts like lists, stacks, and queues, and progressing to more advanced data structures such as linked lists, trees, and graphs. This book also introduces greedy algorithms and dynamic programming–two powerful approaches to solving challenging programming problems.

Each concept is introduced in plain language, with a focus on practical implementation in Python. You'll find clear explanations, code examples, review questions, and practical applications. This book won't make you an expert overnight, but it will give you the tools and confidence to analyze problems more effectively, design smarter solutions, and continue growing as a programmer. Whether you're looking to level up your problem-solving skills or simply write more elegant code, this resource will support you on your path forward.

By the end of this book, you should understand:

- How to work with fundamental data structures and algorithms
- How to design recursive solutions
- How to analyze time and space complexity
- How to implement and apply stacks and queues
- How to use linked lists for dynamic data handling
- How hash tables support efficient data storage and lookup
- How trees represent hierarchical data and support fast search
- How graphs model relationships and enable pathfinding
- How to apply dynamic programming to optimize problems
- How to solve real-world challenges using algorithmic thinking

Who Can Benefit From This Book?

- Learners who have completed an introduction to Python and want to level up
- Students at the high school or undergraduate level studying computer science or related fields
- Professionals looking to deepen their coding skills
- Self-taught programmers who want to strengthen their foundations
- Hobbyists and coders who enjoy tackling real-world problems through code
- Educators seeking an approachable, project-friendly resource

How to Use This Book?

This book is designed to be flexible and adaptable to your learning style and goals, but here are some suggestions to help you get the most out of it:

Start from the beginning

If you're moving on from beginner-level Python, starting with Chapter 1 will help reinforce foundational ideas while setting the stage for more advanced topics. The early chapters introduce key concepts that are further developed as you progress through the book.

Jump into specific topics

If you're already comfortable with some basic data structures, feel free to jump into the more advanced chapters. While the chapters are written sequentially, many of them are self-contained, allowing you to focus on the areas that interest you most. Just be prepared to refer back to earlier sections if something feels unfamiliar.

Practice along the way

Each chapter includes code examples, review questions, and practical applications. If you're using a digital copy, feel free to copy and paste the code, but there's real value in typing it out yourself. Experiment with the provided code and explore your own solutions to the problems.

Regardless of how you choose to use this book, make sure you engage actively with the examples. Algorithmic thinking is a skill you build by doing, not just by reading.

## CHAPTER 1

Introduction to Data Structures and Algorithms

Key Learning Objectives

- Understand what data structures are, along with common examples.
- Understand what algorithms are, along with some common types.
- Gain insight into the role of algorithms and how they are used to solve problems.

This chapter covers the fundamental aspects of data structures and algorithms, two important concepts to help move programmers from beginner coders to more experienced programmers. We will investigate what exactly a data structure is and how we have been using them all along. We will also look at what algorithms are, why they are important, and what they are used for.

1.1 What are Data Structures?

As a simple definition, data structures are ways of organizing and storing data. This is an extremely open definition, and can be applied to almost everything that we do as programmers. After all, regardless of whether we are programming an application, a game, or a data science project, there will be data that needs to be handled. As programmers in the Python® language, we use data structures in most, if not all, of our programs.

1.1.1 Primitive Data Structures

In general, we can group data structures into two categories: primitive data structures and non-primitive data structures. Primitive data structures are the basic data types like integers, floats, and booleans.

Integers are ideal for counting discrete quantities and for indexing sequences. An added benefit is that they require less memory than non-discrete numeric types. For simple true/false conditions, booleans are even more efficient. They are ideal for representing logical states upon which conditional expressions and conditional statements depend, allowing us to determine the program's flow of control. In many programming languages, booleans require less memory than integers. Floats have their own benefits where fractional values are required.

Programming wouldn't be practical if we were limited to working with primitive data structures alone. While primitive data structures won't be the primary focus of this book, understanding their characteristics and limitations is a valuable first step toward making thoughtful choices when working with more complex, non-primitive data structures.

1.1.2 Non-Primitive Data Structures

Non-primitive data structures are more complex and allow for more sophisticated data management.[1] Python has some data structures included, which we use regularly. These include lists, tuples, sets, and dictionaries. There are other data structures that can be utilized by computer programmers, which will be discussed throughout the chapters of this book. These include stacks, queues, linked lists, trees, and graphs. In order to streamline things, we will simply refer to non-primitive data structures as data structures.

Each data structure lends itself to its own set of uses. Imagine we were building a to-do list app using built-in Python data structures for illustration. We would want to store data in a way that was ordered and could be modified as we add and remove tasks. It wouldn't make sense to use sets as they are unordered or tuples since they cannot be changed.

When writing programs, we need to evaluate our potential data structures to consider the best tool for the task.

1.1.3 Abstract data types

In addition to the built-in data structures, we can also create abstract data types, also known as ADTs. ADTs focus on the behavior and operations of a data structure. By ignoring the language-specific implementations, programmers can focus on how to use them to solve problems. Once we do start implementing ADTs, we can keep the code modular, making it easier to debug, test, and maintain.

---

1. A. Padma Reddy, Data Structures and Algorithms Using C++ (Chennai: SciTech Publications, 2009), 5–8.

The implementation of an ADT is built on top of existing data structures provided by the programming language and, sometimes, previously defined ADTs. Many ADTs in Python are built on top of lists. For example, a stack adds and removes objects from the top of the stack. In Python, they may be based on lists using the `append()` method to push items onto the stack and the `pop()` method to remove objects from the stack.

An alternative representation of a stack might employ an array instead of a list, using a cursor (an index to the top of the stack). Once an ADT is defined and implemented, it can be reused in multiple programs. Additional functions can be added to the data structure without requiring the rest of the program to be rewritten, making the code modular. Most of the data structures discussed in this book will be abstract data types.

Through this book, we will be investigating a variety of ADTs. Stacks, as briefly mentioned, are a collection of elements that follow the Last In, First Out (LIFO) principle. When a new item is added to the top of the list, the existing items become deeper relative to the top. When an object is retrieved, the top item is removed for use, and the item immediately below it becomes the new top of the stack. This is illustrated in Figure 1.1. It's a bit like products on a grocery store shelf. Unless the stock is rotated, the items at the back of the shelf have been there the longest, and the item at the front, which was the last one placed, will be the one the customer selects.

Figure 1.1 Adding and removing an item from a stack

New Elements
Added at Top

Elements Accessed
and Removed from Top

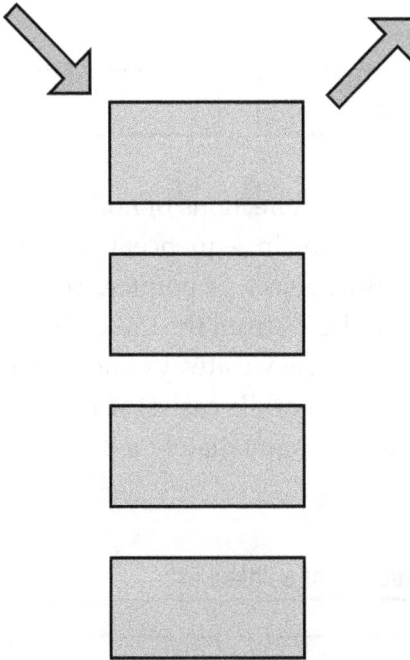

Queues are similar to stacks, but work on the First In, First Out (FIFO) principle. New elements are added to the back of the queue, and retrieved items come from the front of the queue. This is like waiting in line at a store. The customer in the front has been there the longest and will be the next served. In fact, this is known as a queue in England.

Figure 1.2 Adding and removing an item from a queue

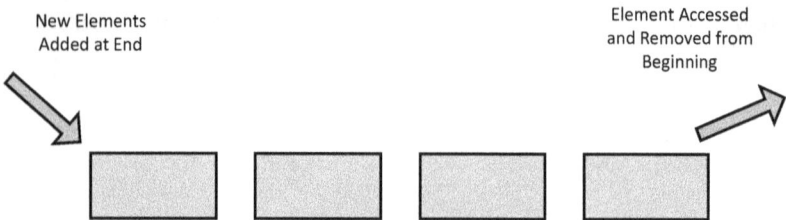

New Elements
Added at End

Element Accessed
and Removed from
Beginning

Linked lists are linear collections of nodes where each node points to the next one in sequence. Each node holds an element such as a value, object, or pointer. This also allows us to add and remove items from the linked list without locating it in memory, since we always know where the next item is. It's a bit like the world's easiest scavenger hunt. Once we find one item, it immediately tells us where the next item is.

Figure 1.3 The structure of a linked list

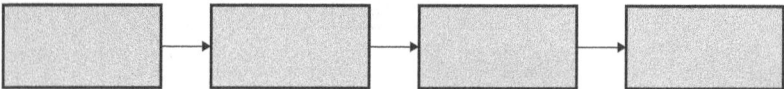

Trees are hierarchical structures that consist of nodes connected by edges. Each node has data and may have any number of child nodes. The top node of the tree is known as the root. Each node connects to zero or more child nodes. A node that has child nodes is called the parent of its child nodes. A node with no children is called a leaf node. Trees are great for organizing data. Consider the way files are organized! A directory is a kind of file that may have child files. Each child file may be a file containing data or another directory. Data files have no children and are leaves within the directory structure. At the top of the directory structure, we have the root directory. It's structured a lot like a family tree, showing all the descendants of a single root ancestor.

Figure 1.4 **The structure of a tree**

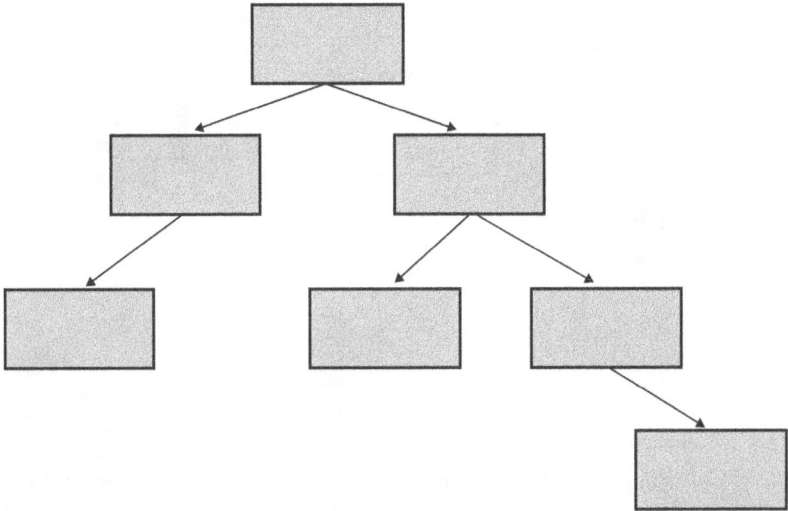

We will also look at graphs which, like trees, are collections of nodes and edges. The main difference is that, unlike trees, graphs do not have a root. With a family tree, it makes sense to have a single starting point, but with a road map, any location is a potential starting point. In a graph, each node keeps a reference to the other nodes that they are connected to. Graphs are more complex and flexible than trees, but can model complex relationships such as the connectedness of social networks.

Figure 1.5 The structure of a graph

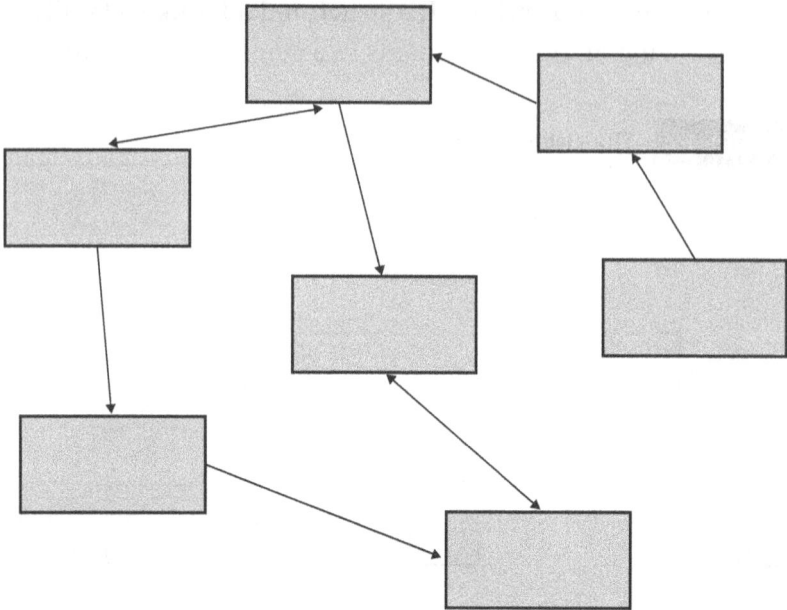

The effectiveness of a program often depends on how the data structures used are suited to the problem the program attempts to solve. Using an ill-suited data structure can cause a program to use more memory than necessary or take considerably longer to run than needed.[2] The amount of memory required is referred to as space complexity, while the amount of time required is, not surprisingly, called time complexity. We will look at how these complexities are measured and how they impact the efficiency of programs in more detail in Chapter 2.

Time and space complexity may not be the biggest concerns for novice programmers, but as our knowledge of programming grows, it is not only important to write

---

2. Thomas H. Cormen et al., *Introduction to Algorithms*, 4th ed. (Cambridge, MA: MIT Press, 2022), 9.

programs that are functional, but also that are efficient. By mastering data structures, programmers can make informed decisions that will allow them to optimize their code for lower memory usage and faster runtime. This can drastically improve the performance of larger applications, where inefficiencies can quickly add up.

1.2 What are Algorithms?

An algorithm is a step-by-step set of instructions designed to perform a specific task or solve a problem. Algorithms work along with data structures to handle and manipulate data. While it is true that all programs follow step-by-step instructions, not all programs are algorithms, nor are all parts of a program an algorithm.

Algorithms should follow some key principles. For instance, algorithms should be clearly defined, have a finite number of steps, take in at least one input, and produce at least one output. Each step of the algorithm should be simple enough to be carried out in a reasonable amount of time.

Algorithms are not unique to programming and can be found everywhere in our daily lives. They help us structure tasks so they can be repeated, optimized, or adapted. Following a recipe for baking a pie, for example, can be considered an algorithm. There is a defined sequence of steps from mixing the dry ingredients, adding the wet ingredients, rolling out the dough, adding the filling, and baking the pie at a certain temperature for a certain amount of time. Each step must be completed in the correct order, or we risk not getting a pie as our output. There may be slight differences in the path through the algorithm depending on the exact details of the parameters, but the overall algorithm itself won't change.

For example, if we want to bake five pies, we would have to change the amount of ingredients used and may need to split up tasks differently than if we were only baking one pie. We might have to use slightly different amounts of flour based on the humidity of the room. Likewise, algorithms may run slightly differently based on the parameters passed into them. Expanding on our pie example, a family recipe might be scalable to create five or ten pies, but it may not be efficient for mass production. Just like there are many apple pie recipes, there are often different algorithms for the same task. There may not be a best algorithm, but there may be one that is best for the given situation.

Algorithms are the driving logic behind the functionality of a program. They dictate how data is processed, manipulated, and used to achieve the outcome. An algorithm can be as simple as a process to sort a list of numbers in ascending order or as complex as a pathfinding algorithm to find the quickest route to your destination. In more advanced cases, such as artificial intelligence or machine learning, algorithms can adapt and learn from data, making decisions based on patterns they identify.

While there are many types of algorithms, some key types of algorithms include sorting algorithms, search algorithms, and pathfinding algorithms.

- Sorting algorithms are used to arrange data in a specific order, which is an important starting point for many other algorithms. Python already has methods for sorting, but examining different ways to sort is a great way to understand the details of efficient algorithms.

- Search algorithms help efficiently locate items within a collection, typically one that is already sorted. Again, Python has methods for doing this; however, the practice of exploring these algorithms is an important step in understanding the different ways to approach the same problem. It is also important because the built-in Python methods may not work for the data structures we will write ourselves.

- Pathfinding algorithms will be an important type of algorithm to investigate when we look at graphs in Chapter 8. Pathfinding algorithms focus on finding the shortest route between nodes, which is very important when looking at navigation, but also has applications in video games and networking.

In daily life, we often use simplified methods to solve problems, even if they do not give an exact result. This is especially common when performing mental math. To convert temperatures from Celsius to Fahrenheit, we can use the "human algorithm," i.e., multiply the Celsius by two, and add thirty. This gives us a very quick, simple value which would be close enough for most cases, even though it isn't fully accurate. A more exact algorithm would be to multiply the Celsius temperature by nine-fifths and then add thirty-two. This would give us a more accurate value, but for most people, this would take longer to complete.

Figure 1.6 Equations for converting Celsius to Fahrenheit

$$F \approx 2 \times C + 30 \qquad F = \frac{9}{5} \times C + 32$$

Algorithms are all about trade-offs, and while there tend to be many ways to solve problems, what's the "best" solution often depends on the situation. The trade-offs typically involve time complexity (the speed at which it runs) and space complexity (the memory it uses).

that any tradesperson would require. Likewise, a backend developer, a data scientist, and a generative artist would all use different algorithms in their daily workflow. Instead of focusing on one specific group of programmers, we will explore algorithms that have common principles that underpin algorithmic thinking.

Understanding algorithms also helps build soft skills associated with programming. It sharpens our program-solving abilities and critical thinking skills. This book will serve as a resource for learning about adaptation and efficiency, allowing us to progress into specialized areas of programming.

And then there's the elephant in the room: the technical interview. While studying algorithms certainly sharpens a programmer's coding skills and critical thinking, the primary reason many people pick up a book on algorithms is to prepare for those high-stakes interviews. Although this book isn't designed specifically as an interview prep guide, the algorithms covered are among the most commonly referenced in technical interviews. That said, simply memorizing algorithms is not a helpful tactic. Questions are often designed with specific algorithms in mind; however, it is the application that interviewers are interested in. The algorithm is simply the starting point for the problem, not the solution.

For example, if an interviewer asked, "Given an unsorted array of integers, find the pair of numbers that add up to a given target sum." There are many ways to solve the problem. Typically, programmers, especially those with less experience, will approach problems with brute-force methods. These involve checking every possible outcome and comparing the results. This will get the right answer, but typically it is not the most efficient way of approaching the problem.

In pseudocode, a brute-force approach to this problem would look like this.

```
for i from 0 to length(arr) - 1:
  for j from i + 1 to length(arr) - 1:
    if arr[i] + arr[j] == target:
      print("Pair found:", arr[i], arr[j])
        return
print("No pair found")
```

For a small set of values, this approach could be valid, but as the list of numbers grows, the number of comparisons would also grow dramatically. A more efficient approach would be to use a set, which is a collection of unique items. For each number in the array, we can calculate the complementary value required to reach the target. If this number is in our seen set, then we have the two values that add up to the target. If not, then we add the value to the seen set and move to the next value. This dramatically reduces the amount of comparisons needed for large lists of values, but keep in mind we also need to check through our set, which grows large with time.

```
initialize an empty set seen

for each number num in arr:
  complement = target - num
    if complement is in seen:
      print("Pair found:", num, complement)
        return
    add num to seen
print("No pair found")
```

Figure 1.7 Solving the problem using a set

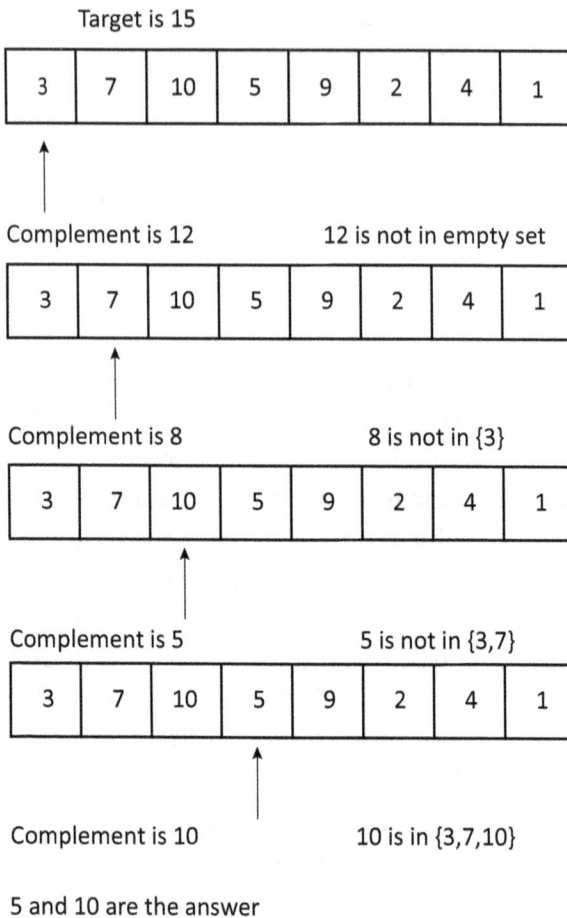

Target is 15

3	7	10	5	9	2	4	1

Complement is 12   12 is not in empty set

3	7	10	5	9	2	4	1

Complement is 8   8 is not in {3}

3	7	10	5	9	2	4	1

Complement is 5   5 is not in {3,7}

3	7	10	5	9	2	4	1

Complement is 10   10 is in {3,7,10}

5 and 10 are the answer

If we are aware of common algorithms, we can use a sorting algorithm to first sort the list of values. While sorting takes time, many sorting algorithms are very efficient and can be an excellent first step to solving a problem. Once sorted, we can assign pointers to the first and last numbers, that is the smallest and largest numbers to see what the sum is. If it's the target, we are done, but this is unlikely. If the sum is less than the target we move the first pointer to the second value and try again, otherwise we move the last pointer to the next highest value. By continuing this process, we will either quickly find the target, or our pointers will meet telling us that there is no way to get the target.

```
#Implement an efficient sorting algorithm
sort(arr)

#Initialize two pointers
left = 0
right = length(arr) - 1

#Iterate while left pointer is less than
#right pointer

while left < right:
    current_sum = arr[left] + arr(right)
    if current_sum == target:
        print("Pair found:", arr[left], arr[right])
            return
    else if current_sum < target:
        left = left + 1
        #Move the left pointer to the right
    else:
        right = right - 1
        #Move the right pointer to the left

print("No pair found")
```

Keep in mind that while Figure 1.8 may look longer, there is no growing set to compare values against, which can make it fairly efficient for long lists. However, the need to sort the array at the beginning should be taken into consideration before choosing the "best" algorithm for this task.

In this case, the pointer algorithm has more steps than the set algorithm. For short lists, the set algorithm is quicker since the values do not have to be sorted first. Unfortunately, with a larger list, the set algorithm will become less efficient since we could have a very large set to work through. The pointer algorithm can be slower for a small list since we have to sort it and then start working our way in from both ends. For a large list, the time lost sorting is much less than the time it would take to check our set over and over again. So, which is the "best" algorithm? It really depends on the exact nature of the input list.

Figure 1.8 Solving the problem using sorting and two pointers

Target is 15

3	7	10	5	9	2	4	1

Sort the list first

1	2	3	4	5	7	9	10

1 + 10 = 11
11 is less than 15
so move the first pointer

1	2	3	4	5	7	9	10

2 + 10 = 12
12 is less than 15
so move the first pointer

Checking 3 and 10 gives 13, so move pointer 1
Checking 4 and 10 gives 14, so move pointer 1

1	2	3	4	5	7	9	10

5 + 10 = 15
We found 15,
so 5 and 10 are the answer

The impact of algorithms extends far beyond just the code that we will write as programmers. They power countless real-world applications, from basic automation to complex decision-making systems. In our daily lives, algorithms are the force behind search engines retrieving the most relevant information, social media platforms suggesting content, and e-commerce websites recommending products based on our buying behavior. Our world is increasingly dependent on algorithms, and yet many of us are unaware of what algorithms truly are and how they function.

In modern healthcare, where every second counts, algorithms can help with diagnostics and creating treatment plans, especially when paired with machine learning. Due to the high amount of data and the importance of prompt results, efficiency is not the goal, it is a necessity.

Financial fraud is a significant issue with bank fraud losses totaling nearly $1.6 billion in 2022.[3] With the ability to process large amounts of data in real time, algorithms can be used to flag suspicious transactions. Algorithms have also been designed to analyze risk management in lending and trading.

Navigation systems analyze traffic patterns, road closures, and user data to determine the shortest, fastest, or most fuel-efficient route to a destination. Without efficient algorithms, these systems would not be able to respond to the real-time data flow. Autonomous vehicles also depend on complex algorithms to make decisions about speed, direction, and obstacle avoidance.

The vast amount of data collected by streaming services would be useless without efficient algorithms to process them. Whether it is for providing recommendations to users

---

3. SEON, *Global Banking Fraud Index 2023*, accessed October 18, 2024, https://seon.io/resources/global-banking-fraud-index-2023/.

or suggesting new content that would appeal to the general public, algorithms are key to the entertainment industry.

The benefit of understanding algorithms goes beyond efficient code. Learning algorithms can help with planning and writing modular code, as it is all about breaking down problems into manageable steps. This benefit extends beyond programming. Who wouldn't want the ability to reduce seemingly impossible life problems into smaller, more manageable ones?

Knowledge of algorithms is an important aspect of the hiring process. Companies are not just looking for people who can program, they are looking for excellent problem solvers. Coding interviews may not focus on specific algorithms, but they will tend to present problems that are best solved using common algorithms. Even when they are not based on a common algorithm, demonstrating algorithmic thinking can set programmers apart in competitive fields. This can open doors to positions in software development, data science, and AI research.

As the world continues to become more data-driven, algorithms will continue to play a critical role in our lives. Whether it is in the areas of artificial intelligence and machine learning, or the Internet of Things, algorithms will play an important role. Understanding how algorithms shape fields such as finance and healthcare will help programmers not only write efficient code but also understand the larger implications of their work.

Chapter Summary

- Data structures are ways of organizing and storing data, and they can be classified as either primitive or non-primitive data structures.

- Abstract data types (ADTs) focus on the data structure's behavior and operations rather than its implementation.

- Algorithms are sets of instructions for performing tasks and solving problems.

- There is no single "best" algorithm, but some are simply more efficient for specific situations.

Quiz

1. **Which is the best definition of a data structure?**

    a. A programming language used in data science
    b. A step-by-step process for solving a problem
    c. A type of algorithm used for sorting data
    d. A way to organize and store data

2. **What is the main difference between primitive and non-primitive data structures?**

    a. Non-primitive data structures are built into Python, while primitive ones are not.
    b. Non-primitive data structures are more efficient than primitive ones.
    c. Primitive data structures are basic data types, while non-primitive ones are not.
    d. Primitive data structures are only used in low-level programming languages.

3. **Which is not a primitive data structure?**

    a. Boolean
    b. Float
    c. Integer
    d. List

4. **What is an Abstract Data Type (ADT)?**

    a. A data structure that focuses on behavior and operations
    b. A data structure that focuses on implementation details
    c. A data structure that is always built on top of arrays
    d. A data structure that is specific to the Python programming language

5. **Which data structure follows the Last-In, First-Out (LIFO) principle?**
   a. Linked list
   b. Queue
   c. Stack
   d. Tree

6. **What is the key difference between a tree and a graph?**
   a. Graphs do not have a root node, while trees always do.
   b. Graphs have a hierarchical structure, while trees do not.
   c. Trees can have multiple root nodes, while graphs only have one.
   d. Trees do not have a root node, while graphs always do.

7. **What is space complexity?**
   a. The amount of time an algorithm takes to run
   b. The amount of memory an algorithm requires
   c. The difficulty of understanding an algorithm
   d. The number of lines of code in an algorithm

8. **Why is studying sorting algorithms beneficial even though Python has built-in sorting methods?**
   a. It helps in understanding algorithm efficiency and writing custom sorting algorithms.
   b. It is not beneficial, as the Python methods are sufficient.
   c. It is only necessary for programmers who work in low-level languages.
   d. It is required for all data science and machine learning applications.

9. Why is understanding when and why to use specific algorithms important?
    a. It allows programmers to solve problems efficiently.
    b. It ensures that all programmers write code in the same way.
    c. It is only important for passing technical interviews.
    d. It is not important, as all algorithms have the same efficiency.

10. How does the study of algorithms contribute to a programmer's soft skills?
    a. It develops creativity and design sense.
    b. It enhances problem-solving and critical thinking skills.
    c. It improves communication and teamwork abilities.
    d. It teaches effective management skills.

Answer Key

1 – d	2 – c	3 – d	4 – a	5 – c
6 – a	7 – b	8 – a	9 – a	10 – b

## CHAPTER 2

Complexity and Big O Notation

Key Learning Objectives

- Analyze time and space complexity.
- Identify common growth rates and how they apply to algorithms.
- Understand the difference between Big O, Theta, and Omega notation.
- Evaluate the use of recursion and the associated tradeoffs.

This chapter covers the methods of measuring algorithm complexity. Complexity is broken down into two main components: time complexity and space complexity, both of which need to be considered in order to write efficient algorithms. The technique of writing recursive functions will also be investigated.

2.1 Analyzing Complexity

When programmers first learn to write programs, complexity is typically not a major issue. We might write a program that cycles through a list of a dozen items, and even if it is inefficient, the total amount of time and memory involved will not be high. If that list grows larger into the millions, the inefficiencies could become apparent, taking hours or even days to run the program. Novice programmers need to become good at writing code that runs, but developing programmers need to write code that performs well.

We need a way of measuring the efficiency of the programs we write. Complexity analysis helps us understand the efficiency of algorithms by determining how the execution time and memory usage change as the input size changes. This allows us to predict the performance of programs, optimize resource use, and compare various algorithms.

2.1.1 Time Complexity

Time complexity measures how the execution time of an algorithm changes with the size of the input. One thing that tends to confuse newcomers to the field of complexity is that we are not concerned with how long the program takes to run. Rather, we are concerned with the execution time's growth rate as we change the input size. Using a non-programming example, if we were writing a name, it would take us longer to write a longer name than to write a shorter name. Regardless of how long it takes to write a single letter, writing two letters would take roughly twice as long, and three letters would take three times as long. We would consider this to be a linear growth rate since, as the input size increases, the time required increases by a set rate. Table 2.1 shows some of the common growth rates.

| Table 2.1 | Common growth rates |

Growth Rate	Description	Chart
Constant	The runtime doesn't change with the input size.	
Linear	The runtime grows proportionally to the input size.	
Quadratic	The runtime grows quadratically. As the input size doubles, the runtime increases four times.	
Cubic	The runtime grows cubically. As the input size doubles, the runtime increases eight times.	

(*continued*)

Growth Rate	Description	Chart
Logarithmic	The runtime starts high but grows slowly with input size.	

If we were at a meet and greet and every person had to spend a set amount of time talking to every other person, we would see that the number of pairings increases quickly as the number of participants increases. If we invited five people, we would need to schedule 10 meetings. If we double the number of invited people to ten, there would be 45 meetings, an increase of just over four times. As before, this doesn't tell us how long the event will take for either five or ten people. It does give us an idea as to how the time requirements for the event will change as we increase the number of people involved. This can tell us if this is an appropriate format for our event, and help us see how we might want to change things to make it more efficient for everyone involved.

2.1.2 Space Complexity

Much like time complexity, space complexity is a measure of how the memory requirements of an algorithm change based on the input size. What the algorithm does with the information affects space complexity more than the size of the input. Algorithms that reuse or process data in place tend to have low space complexity, while those that create additional structures will tend to have a higher space complexity.

If we had a grocery list and wanted to create a new list of all the items we couldn't get at the store, we would be building a new data structure. The longer our original list is, the longer the new list might be. The space complexity would be linear. As the length of the original list doubles, the length of the new list might double as well.

Figure 2.1 | **Grocery list as an analogy for space complexity**

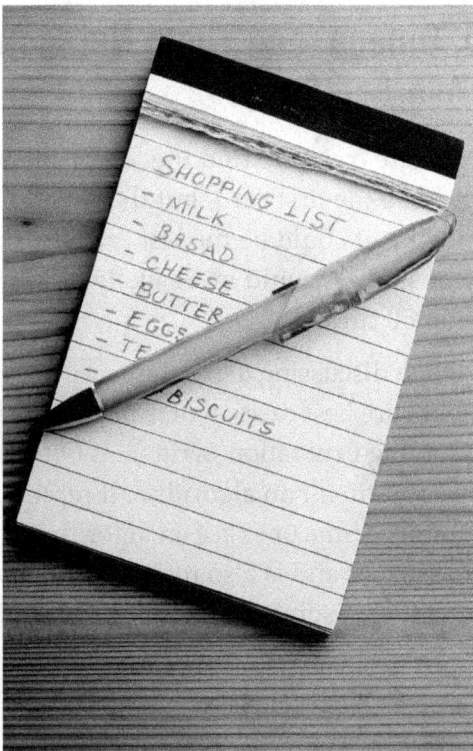

Source: *Torbjørn Helgesen, Unsplash, accessed November 12, 2024, https://unsplash.com/photos/a-green-pen-sitting-on-top-of-a-piece-of-paper-KXfiLwOHrvU.*

If we decided instead to edit the list itself by crossing out purchased items, then this would be the equivalent of editing a list in place. In-place modifications may need to temporarily store some information, so there could be a small amount of storage required; however, there is no dependence on the size of the list. This would make it a constant space complexity.

Even though space complexity may not seem like a major issue compared to time complexity, it becomes an important consideration as we move through our study of algorithms. There is often a trade-off between time efficiency and space efficiency, and both are equally important to consider.

2.2 Big O, Omega, and Theta Notation: Worst, Best, and Average Cases

Imagine we were trying to find the ace of spades in a deck of cards. It could be the first card, but that would be unlikely. If we were unlucky, it could be the last card. In a deck of 52 cards, the ace of spades would more likely be somewhere among the other 50 cards.

Similarly, when discussing algorithms, we need to keep in mind that there are best cases, worst cases, and average cases to consider. Big O notation, written as O(f(n)), describes the worst-case scenario for an algorithm. It represents the maximum amount of time or space an algorithm could require as the input size grows and is also referred to as the upper bound. Table 2.2 shows some common Big O notations.

Table 2.2 Common Big O notations

Constant	O(1)
Linear	O(n)
Quadratic	O(n^2)
Cubic	O(n^3)
Logarithmic	O(log n)

Big O notation is widely used in algorithm analysis because it gives a realistic expectation of how an algorithm will perform. While it is the most common, two other methods of algorithm analysis are also used: Omega notation and Theta notation.

- Omega notation, written as $\Omega(f(n))$, is the lower bound. It is a measure of how the algorithm will perform in the best-case scenario. Omega notation isn't typically used on its own since the best case usually doesn't give a realistic impression of how well the algorithm will perform.

- Theta notation, written as $\Theta(f(n))$, is described as a tight bound. It is a measure of how the algorithm will perform on average. Theta notation takes both the Big O notation and Omega notation into consideration. Table 2.3 shows a sampling of Omega and Theta notations.

Table 2.3   Common Omega and Theta notations

Growth Rate	Omega Notation	Theta Notation
Constant	$\Omega(1)$	$\Theta(1)$
Linear	$\Omega(n)$	$\Theta(n)$
Quadratic	$\Omega(n^2)$	$\Theta(n^2)$
Cubic	$\Omega(n^3)$	$\Theta(n^3)$
Logarithmic	$\Omega(\log n)$	$\Theta(\log n)$

Let's return to our card-finding example and consider the time complexity. If we have 52 cards in a deck, in the best case, we'll find it first. Even if we doubled the deck to 104 cards and were looking for one specific card, in the best case, we'll find it first. No matter how many cards there are, with the right luck, it only takes one try to find the card. We say the Omega notation is $\Omega(1)$, or constant. In the worst-case scenario, with 52 cards, we would have to try all of them, up to the 52nd card. In 104 cards, the worst case would be the 104th try. We double the cards and double the attempts needed, so the Big O notation is linear or O(n).

The average case is a little trickier. If the best case is the first one and the worst case is the last, then on average, we should find it around the middle card. This means for 52 cards, it would be the 26th try. Similarly, for 104 cards, it would be the 52nd try. This growth rate is also linear, since doubling the number of cards also doubles the number of tries necessary to find the correct card on average. Therefore, the Theta notation is Θ(n).

Figure 2.2 shows the growth of the best, worst, and average cases. Again, we must remind ourselves that the rate of change is the important part, not the individual values.

Figure 2.2 **Time Complexity of finding one specific card in a set of cards**

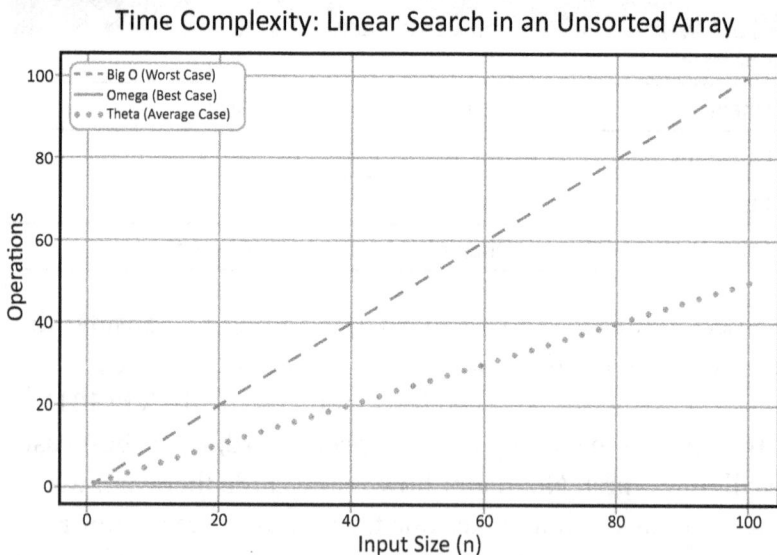

Time Complexity: Linear Search in an Unsorted Array

Let's look at a code-specific example.

```python
from random import randint

def reach_goal(target):
    total_score = 0
    rolls = 0

    while total_score < target:
        roll = randint(1, 6)
        total_score += roll
        rolls += 1

    return rolls
```

Here we have a dice game where we want to roll a target amount. If our target is 6, we should be able to see that the best case would be one roll of six. The worst case would be six rolls of one. Since the average dice roll is mathematically 3.5, the average case would be somewhere around 2 rolls.

Stepping up our game to hit a total of 12, the best we can hope for is two rolls of six. The worst would be 12 rolls of one. Using our average value of 3.5, the average case would be somewhere around 4 rolls. Table 2.4 continues this trend, and Figure 2.3 shows a greatly extended graph.

| Table 2.4 | Best, worst, and average cases for the number of dice rolls to hit a target |

Target	Best Case (all 6s)	Worst Case (all 1s)	Average (average of 3.5)
6	1	6	2 (1.71)
12	2	12	4 (3.43)
24	3	24	7 (6.86)
30	4	30	9 (8.57)
36	5	36	11 (10.29)

| Figure 2.3 | Best, worst, and average cases for the number of dice rolls to hit a target |

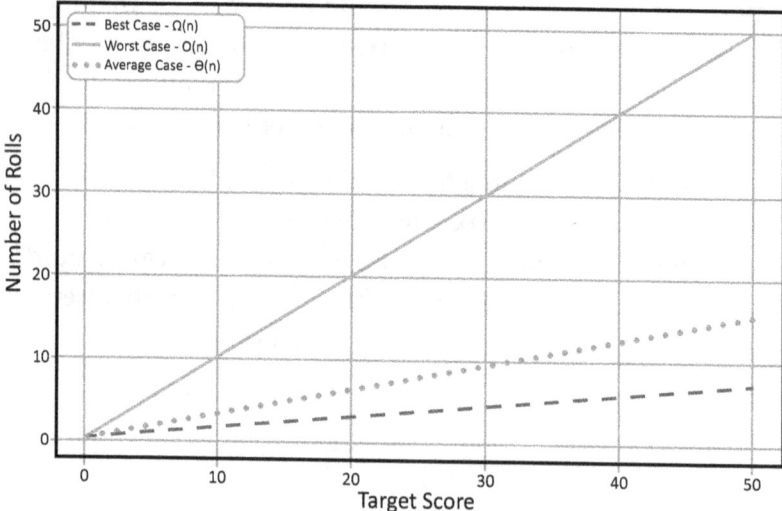

Theoretical Best, Worst, and Average Cases for Dice Rolls

Before moving on, there are still two important things to discuss. First, note how we ignored most of the code in our discussion of complexity. We were really only worried about the number of loops we would take in the while loop. Setting the score and total to zero is a constant operation and doesn't add to the overall time growth. Likewise, returning the value at the end is constant and has no impact when compared to the while loop. We call the while loop a bottleneck in that it is the part of the code that will limit the speed at which it can execute. We tend to focus on the largest growth factor when dealing with complexity.

We also ignored space complexity in this example. The function uses some memory to store variables like `total_ score`, `rolls`, and `roll`, but this memory usage doesn't scale with the number of loops to hit the target. This means the space complexity is constant or O(1). In this case, and many cases, there is no difference between the best, worst, and average cases. As a result, focusing on Big O notation is usually sufficient when considering space complexity, although there will be times when it is helpful to look at the others too.

2.3 Trade-offs Between Recursion and Iteration

2.3.1 Recursion

Recursion is a technique where a function calls itself during its execution. At first glance, it can be a challenging abstraction. However, recursion is extremely powerful and not too difficult to get used to. Figure 2.4 shows a generative artwork using recursion in its creation. Each branch draws another set of smaller branches, which draw another set of branches, which draw another set of branches, until a minimum size is reached. This minimum size is a stopping condition, known as a base case. Through recursion, each branch calls for the creation of the next set of branches, making the code neat and tidy.

| Figure 2.4 | A visual representation of recursion |

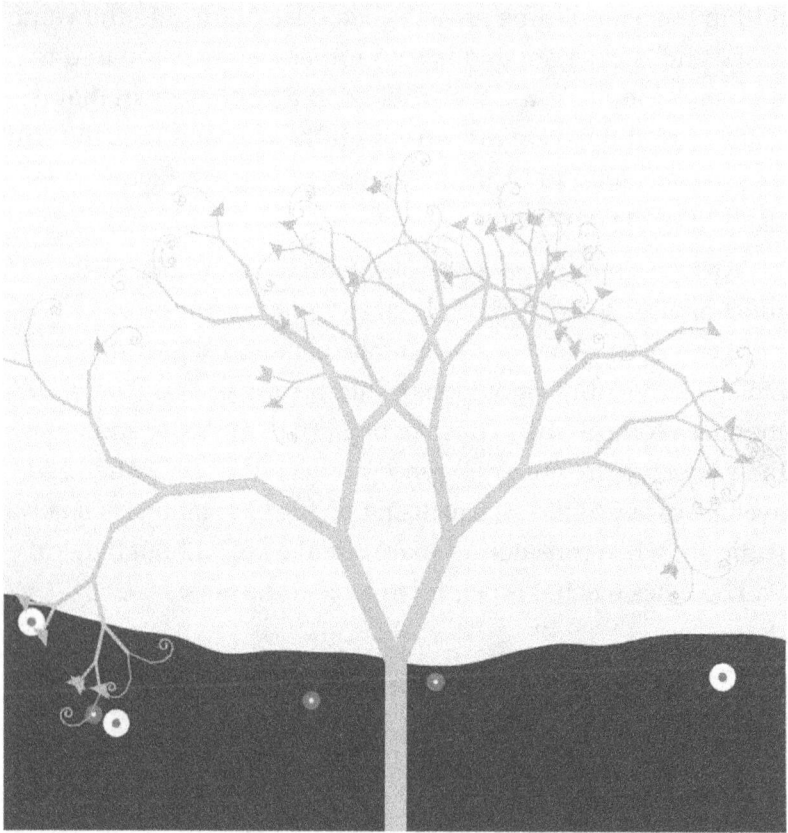

Recursion helps divide a problem into subproblems that can be solved more easily, resulting in simplified code. However, like all good things, recursion has its issues as well. Since each function call will result in new data being created, the space complexity tends to be higher than other methods. By default, Python limits the number of recursive function calls to 1000. This can be overridden, but should be avoided as the increased memory usage could cause a crash. It is seldom necessary to recurse to great depths. When a function recurses deeply, it has likely been poorly written. The repeated function calls can also slow down execution.

The Fibonacci sequence is a famous mathematical sequence where each number is the sum of the two before it.

1, 1, 2, 3, 5, 8, 13, 21, 34, 55.....

Suppose we wanted to write a program to get a particular number off the list. For example, if we wanted to know the fourth number in the Fibonacci sequence. To do this in a traditional iterative manner, we could write a simple for loop.

```
def fibonacci_iterative(n):
  a, b = 0, 1
  for i in range(n):
    #here we set a to b, and
    #set b to the sum of the two values
    a, b = b, a + b
  return a
```

While Python indexes from 0, we will write the code so that passing in 4 will return the fourth term in the sequence. In terms of complexity, we can see that finding the fourth term required four iterations of the loop. Eighth would have required eight iterations. The number of iterations would grow as a function of n and linearly increase our runtime, giving us O(n) time complexity. In terms of space, the variables a and b are created, but they are reused on each iteration. Even the value of i is created and reused. So the space complexity of this function is constant, or O(1).

Now for the recursive version.

```
def fibonacci_recursive(n):
  #base case
  if n <= 1:
    return n
  #recursive call
  return (
    fibonacci_recursive(n - 1)
    + fibonacci_recursive(n - 2)
  )
```

First of all, we have the base case return statement. It is important that the recursion ends at some point, and in this case, it ends when n is less than or equal to 1. Numbers less than 1 are invalid, but it returns a zero, so there is no concern. Returning 1 is important as it is the first and second value of the sequence. Since the value of a number in the Fibonacci sequence is based on the two numbers that come before it, we recursively call for those numbers. Those numbers, in turn, will either be the base case or will recursively call for the two numbers before it. Figure 2.5 illustrates how the value from fibonacci_recursive(4) is determined. Calls to fibonacci_recursive, where n is greater than 1, are decomposed into calls of fibonacci_recursive, on both n-1 and n-2, and the results are returned upward, where they are summed. To compute fibonacci_recursive of 3, we must call fibonacci_recursive of 1 twice. Once to find fibonacci_recursive of 1 and once to find fibonacci_recursive of 2. As you can see, computing a Fibonacci sequence value through recursion requires redundant function calls, and the amount of redundancy increases the higher the value of n.

Figure 2.5 Recursively finding the sixth value in the Fibonacci sequence

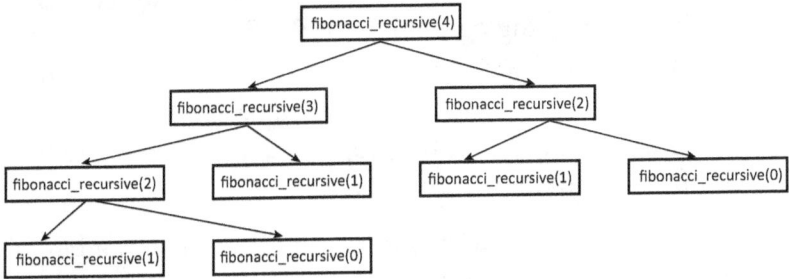

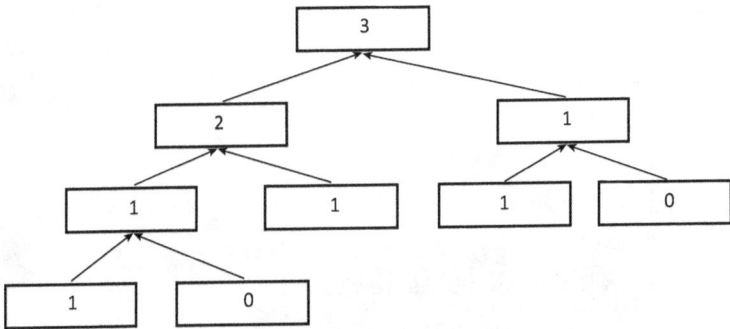

The time complexity of this is not great. In general, each function call creates two more function calls, so we are in an exponential growth situation. This means the time complexity is $O(2^n)$. Exponential time complexities should be avoided at all costs as they can lead to crashes. The space complexity is a little trickier to understand due to the nature of the stack. We will look into stacks as a data structure in Chapter 4. As the recursive calls start adding up, we will get to a depth of 4 before we start returning some values. This would be 4 times the memory required by a single call. Once the values are returned, the memory is freed before more calls are created. If we had, for example, called for the eighth number in the sequence, we would have ended up eight recursions deep before returning, requiring eight times the memory of one call. This is a linear space complexity, O(n).

Recursively writing a function for the Fibonacci sequence, based on our complexity analysis, is a bad idea, but we will explore many different algorithms in this book, some of which benefit from an iterative approach, while others will benefit from recursion.

Prime factorization is the process of breaking a number down into its prime factors. For example, 60 can be factored down to 2 × 2 × 3 × 5. Let's compare approaching this problem from both an iterative and a recursive viewpoint.

```
def prime_factors_iterative(n):
  factors = []
  divisor = 2
  while n > 1:
    # Divide n by the current divisor
    # as long as it is divisible
    while n % divisor == 0:
      factors.append(divisor)
      n //= divisor
    # Move to the next potential divisor
    divisor += 1
    #Stop if divisor exceeds sqrt(n)
    if divisor * divisor > n:
      if n > 1:
        factors.append(n)   # Remaining n is prime
      break
  return factors
```

The logic in the iterative version is that we start with a divisor of 2 and continue dividing by 2 as long as there is no remainder. Once there is no remainder, we increase by one and continue along this path until we pass the square root of our number. This is a common stopping point when factoring, as any factor greater than the square root would have a complementary factor less than the square root, which we already checked. We keep adding the evenly divisible values into our factors list and return the whole list at the end.

```python
def prime_recursive(n, divisor=2):
    # Base case: If n is 1, there are no more factors
    if n == 1:
        return []

    #Stop recursion if divisor exceeds sqrt(n)
    if divisor * divisor > n:
        return [n]  # Remaining n is prime

    # If n is divisible by the current divisor,
    # add it to the factors
    if n % divisor == 0:
        return (
            [divisor]
            + prime_recursive(n // divisor, divisor)
        )

    # Otherwise, move to the next potential divisor
    return prime_recursive(n, divisor + 1)
```

2.3.2 Comparing Recursion and Iteration

One thing that's evident about the recursive version is that it is compact. While the goal is not to write the shortest code, lengthy code is less readable. The logic is the same, but there is not the same amount of nesting, which helps programmers see the steps involved.

In this case, the recursive version wins in terms of readability, but what about time and space complexity?

The iterative version has a time complexity of $O(\sqrt{n})$ where n is the number being factored. In the worst case, for a prime number, we would have to check each number up to the square root of the value. The recursive version has the same time complexity, as it would also check values in the same manner.

The iterative version creates a list of factors that take up additional memory. Larger input values may not necessarily have more factors than smaller input values, so it is not directly related to n. We call this O(k) complexity since it has no relationship to n. Typically, O(k) complexity grows slower than linear.

Then there's the recursive version. Recursive functions tend to lose out when it comes to space complexity due to the stack of function calls, each requiring their own set of values being created. The space complexity of the recursive version is $O(\sqrt{n})$. The worst-case scenario is that the number is prime. For a prime number, we make a recursive call for every number from 2 up to the square root of the value before we exit. This makes the recursive method very resource-hungry for large numbers. Figure 2.6 shows the best and worst-case space complexities versus the actual space complexities. The space requirements are much higher for prime numbers than for composite numbers.

Figure 2.6	Best case [O(log(n))] and worst case [O($\sqrt{n}$)] space complexity for recursive prime factorization

Space Complexity

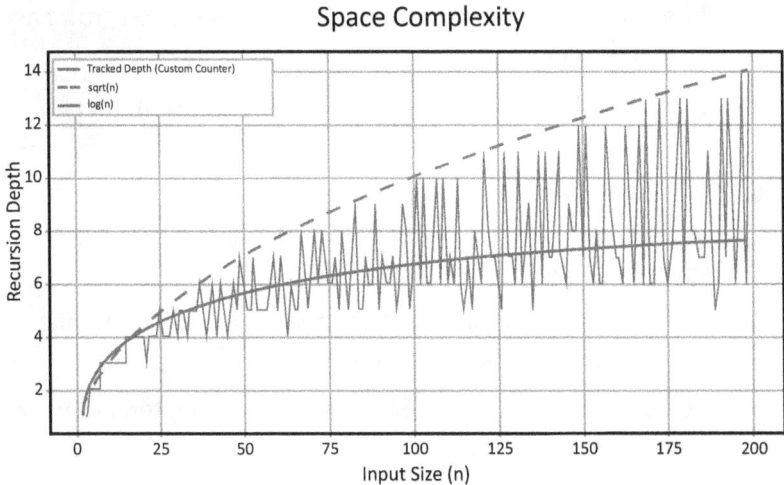

Overall, the iterative version is still the better choice here, but the handling of the loops can create less manageable code. The space complexity makes the iterative version better for large numbers since there are only several factors that need to be stored, not a large number of function calls. That being said, the code simplicity of the recursive version could make it worth using in a project where only small numbers would need to be factorized. Recursion is also a natural fit for the logic of the problem, where we repeatedly divide a number, then divide that number, and so on. This tends to be the general case for iteration versus recursion. Recursion can be a powerful tool to consider when developing algorithms.

Chapter Summary

- Time complexity is a measure of how the execution grows as input size increases.

- Space complexity is a measure of the additional memory used by an algorithm as input size increases.

- Big O notation represents the worst case, whereas Omega notation represents the best case. The average case is represented by Theta notation.

- Recursion functions are functions that call themselves, and they can be a natural solution to many problems.

- Recursive solutions, while often more readable, tend to have high space complexity.

- Choosing between iterative and recursive solutions involves considering trade-offs.

Quiz

1. **What is the major focus of complexity analysis?**
    a. The actual runtime of an algorithm
    b. The growth rate of the runtime and memory usage
    c. The length of code used to write the algorithm
    d. The specifications of the hardware required

2. **Which represents a linear time complexity?**
    a. Doubling input size doubles the runtime
    b. Doubling input size quadruples the runtime
    c. Runtime grows logarithmically with size
    d. Runtime remains constant regardless of input size

3. **What does an algorithm with space complexity O(1) indicate?**
    a. Memory usage grows exponentially with input size
    b. Memory usage grows logarithmically with input size
    c. Memory usage increases with input size
    d. Memory usage remains the same regardless of input size

4. **What does Big-O notation represent?**
    a. Average-case scenario
    b. Best-case scenario
    c. Worst-case scenario
    d. Total memory used

5. **Which notation is used to describe the average-case performance?**

   a. Alpha
   b. Big O
   c. Omega
   d. Theta

6. **Why is Big O notation often preferred over Omega notation?**

   a. It is more practical to prepare for the worst case.
   b. It is the most accurate notation.
   c. It is simpler to calculate.
   d. It represents an average runtime.

7. **What is the main advantage of recursion over iteration?**

   a. It always runs faster than iteration.
   b. It avoids using the call stack.
   c. It can simplify code by solving subproblems.
   d. It uses less memory.

8. **Which complexity would be best for a large input size?**

   a. $O(n^3)$
   b. $O(\log n)$
   c. $O(n^2)$
   d. $O(2^n)$

9. **Why is it important to focus on the largest growth factor in an algorithm's time complexity?**
   a. To calculate the exact runtime
   b. To ensure all operations are considered equally
   c. To keep space complexity low
   d. To simplify analysis and identify bottlenecks

10. **What is the main problem with recursion when compared to iteration?**
    a. Recursion cannot handle complex cases.
    b. Recursion eliminates base cases.
    c. Recursion is always slower.
    d. Recursion requires more memory.

Answer Key

1 – b	2 – a	3 – d	4 – c	5 – d
6 – a	7 – c	8 – b	9 – d	10 – d

Chapter 3

Arrays

Key Learning Objectives

- Understand the differences between static and dynamic arrays.
- Perform fundamental array operations, such as insertion, deletion, searching, traversing, and sorting.
- Analyze the time and space complexity of common operations.
- Implement and compare sorting algorithms and searching algorithms.

In this chapter, we will explore the fundamentals of arrays. Arrays allow us to organize and manipulate collections of data efficiently. While Python does not have traditional static arrays, lists can be used as a reasonable stand-in. Various sorting and searching algorithms will also be explored and compared in terms of their complexity and use cases.

3.1 Introduction to Arrays

In a pure sense, an array is a collection of elements of the same type that are stored in a continuous block of memory. Arrays allow us to store multiple values in a single variable, making it easier to organize and manipulate data. In Python, arrays are typically represented using lists, although there is an array module that can be used to create arrays.

```
import array

arr = array.array('i',[1,2,3,4])
```

The 'i' gives the data type being used for the array. Table 3.1 shows common type codes.

Table 3.1   **Type codes for arrays[4]**

Type Code	Python Type
'i'	int
'f'	float
'w'	Unicode character

Arrays created by the array module differ from lists in a few ways, but the main differences are that they use contiguous memory and are limited to a single data type. They are more efficient, but for the sake of simplicity, we will focus on using lists as a stand-in for arrays.

There are two types of arrays: static and dynamic. A static array has a fixed size and cannot be changed. These are more memory efficient, since the memory use is known; they can be allocated without the need for updating. Static arrays

---

4. Python Software Foundation. *The array module — Python 3.12.0 documentation.* https://docs.python.org/3/library/array.html. Accessed on Nov 28, 2024.

are used in lower-level languages. A dynamic array can be dynamically resized as elements are added or removed. Resizing arrays is a costly operation, as the information may need to be copied to a new location in memory if additional space is required.

Both lists and arrays created by the array module are dynamic arrays. For convenience, we will use lists as a stand-in for arrays when looking at algorithms, although there are some benefits to using arrays instead. Lists can be beneficial due to their ability to handle different types of data. Instead of storing the information in a continuous block of memory, they store references to the location of the data. These references are known as pointers. This implementation makes lists slower to use due to having to update these pointers whenever the data is changed. Table 3.2 shows the main differences between the array types.

Table 3.2   Differences between types of arrays

Feature	True Static Arrays	Python array module	Python list
Homogeneous Data	Yes	Yes	No
Dynamic Resizing	No	Yes	Yes
Memory Layout	Contiguous memory	Contiguous memory	Array of pointers
Fixed Size	Yes	No	No
Performance	Faster for fixed-size usage	Fast, but allows resizing	Slower due to resizing and changing pointer references

There are no true static arrays in Python, but tuples can be used for static-like behavior since their size is fixed. Like lists, however, they actually store pointers to their information.

3.2 Array Operations

There are many operators that are common to most data structures. Regardless of the data structure, we need to be able to insert, delete, search, traverse, and sort the information within the structure. Using Python lists, we do not need to write our own methods to perform these operations, but can rely on the built-in methods.

3.2.1 Insertion

For insertion, we can use `append()` and `insert()`. `remove()` and `pop()` can be used for deletion. We will be implementing algorithms for searching and sorting lists, even though there are built-in methods. By default, searching can be accomplished using the `in` keyword or `index()` if we need to know where in the list the item is. As well, the `sort()` method sorts lists in-place, although we can also use the `sorted()` function. When dealing with other data structures, we will need to implement all of these methods ourselves.

Array operations using built-in list methods tend to be fairly efficient. For example, adding elements to a list using the `append()` method only has a worst-case time complexity of O(1), since we do not need to navigate through the array to add the new data. This is not strictly true, since the addition of an item could require the array to be moved to a new location in memory, but this would typically not be the case. We call this type of analysis the amortized worst case. This is used when there is an absolute worst case that is highly unlikely to happen. The amortized worst case is like the typical worst case. We will not calculate this, but it is a common way that documentation will present complexity.[5]

Inserting an element at a specific position is a more complex operation. The `insert()` method takes two arguments: the index to insert the value, and the value itself. To insert the value, all other values have to be shifted to the right, which is where the complexity comes in. If the item is being inserted at the beginning of the list, then the entire list has to be moved, which is the worst-case situation. This means the amortized complexity would be $O(n)$, where n is the length of the list.

3.2.2 Traversal

When looking at the complexity of algorithms using lists, we typically consider three bottlenecks. The first involves looping through a list. Looping through all items in a list gives a complexity of $O(n)$, since we need to access each one. The longer the list, the longer it will take. A list of 10 items will take twice as long as a list of 5 items.

```
for item of my_list:
    print(item)
```

Having to compare elements of a list against itself has a complexity of $O(n^2)$ since each element is accessed for each other element in turn. A list of 5 items would require 25 operations, while a list of 10 items would require 100 operations.

```
for item1 of my_list:
    for item2 of my_list:
        print(item1, item2)
```

---

5. Python Software Foundation. *Time Complexity in Python.*
https://wiki.python.org/moin/TimeComplexity. Accessed November 28, 2024

If we had two lists of different sizes, we could refer to the complexity as O(m × n), where m and n are the sizes of the two different lists, but the concept is the same.

Finding an item in a list can be done by simply iterating over a list, so it also has a complexity of O(n), but we will investigate ways that we can cut this down, at least for sorted lists.

The sorting of a list is another major bottleneck, which is the focus of many algorithms in the next section. Python's built-in sorting method has a complexity of O(n log n). This is often known as log-linear, and its growth rate, while higher than linear, is nowhere as bad as quadratic. While we won't analyze the complexity, it is a good base for comparison when looking at our own sorting algorithms.

Figure 3.1 **Comparing O(n log n) to linear and quadratic complexity**

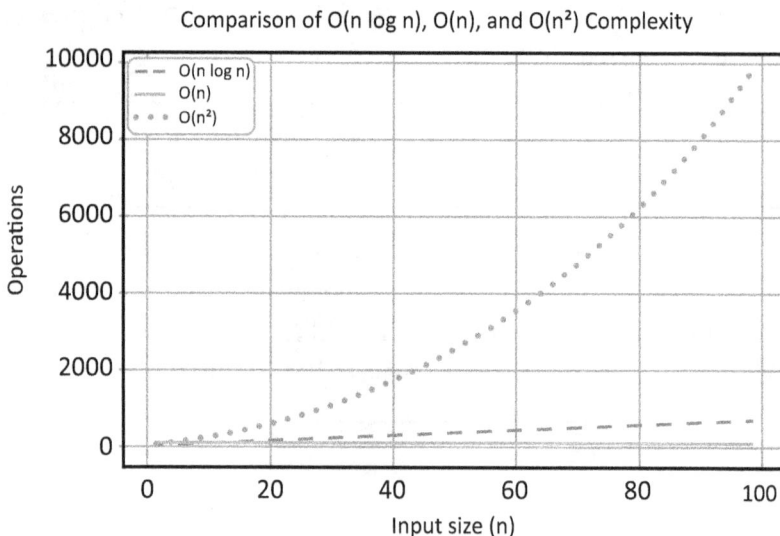

Comparison of O(n log n), O(n), and O(n²) Complexity

3.3 Array-Based Algorithms

3.3.1 Sorting

Sorting is a fundamental operation that can greatly increase the efficiency of data processing, especially when paired with search algorithms. We will investigate selection sort, insertion sort, merge sort, and quicksort, which are commonly studied and utilized algorithms. Each has its own unique characteristics and use cases.

A. Selection Sort

Selection sort is a comparison-based sorting algorithm. It loops through an array and when it finds an unsorted element, it swaps it with the first unsorted element, tracked by a pointer.

In pseudocode:

```
FOR i FROM 0 TO LENGTH(array) - 1:
  min_index = i
  FOR j FROM i + 1 TO LENGTH(array) - 1:
    IF array[j] < array[min_index]:
      min_index = j
  SWAP array[i] WITH array[min_index]
END FOR
```

It can be a little difficult to see all the details in the pseudocode; however, there are a few quick things that we can see. This algorithm is going to have a high complexity due to the nested for loops. Since we are looping through the list again for each element, we have a time complexity of $O(n^2)$. There is no way to exit the loops, so the best case, worst case, and average complexity are all the same. This is because the algorithm always goes completely through each loop regardless of the input.

Recall that the built-in sort has a complexity of O(n log n), so this method is less efficient. There are no additional arrays being created, so we consider the space complexity O(1) since we only need to store the same number of variables regardless of the size of the array. This is the same as the built-in method. Figure 3.2 illustrates the process.

Figure 3.2 An example of selection sort

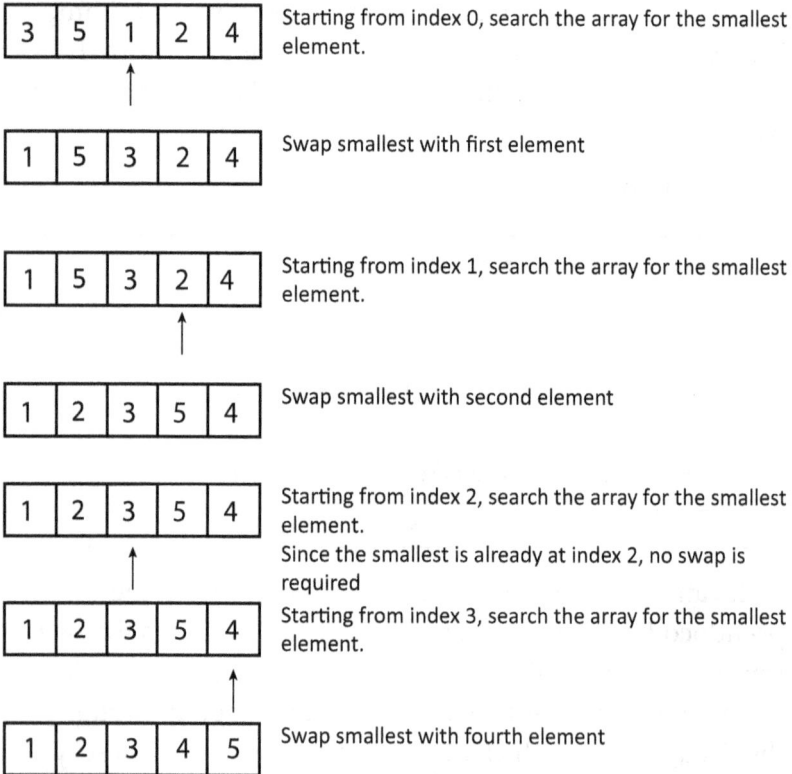

| 3 | 5 | 1 | 2 | 4 |

Starting from index 0, search the array for the smallest element.

| 1 | 5 | 3 | 2 | 4 |

Swap smallest with first element

| 1 | 5 | 3 | 2 | 4 |

Starting from index 1, search the array for the smallest element.

| 1 | 2 | 3 | 5 | 4 |

Swap smallest with second element

| 1 | 2 | 3 | 5 | 4 |

Starting from index 2, search the array for the smallest element.
Since the smallest is already at index 2, no swap is required

| 1 | 2 | 3 | 5 | 4 |

Starting from index 3, search the array for the smallest element.

| 1 | 2 | 3 | 4 | 5 |

Swap smallest with fourth element

The implementation in Python is fairly straightforward and follows the pseudocode almost directly.

```
def selection_sort(arr):
  n = len(arr)
  for i in range(n):
    min_index = i
    # Find the minimum element,
    # ignoring elements before i
    for j in range(i + 1, n):
      if arr[j] < arr[min_index]:
        min_index = j
    # Swap the minimum element with the first
    # unsorted element
    arr[i], arr[min_index] = arr[min_index], arr[i]
  return arr
```

If selection sort is so inefficient, why include it here? Many times when developing an algorithm, programmers may default to a brute force method. Brute forcing methods do solve the problem in a logical way, but typically in an inefficient way. We can find ways to improve upon our methods by first looking at the brute force solution. It makes sense to loop through the list to see which value is the smallest and then move it to the front; however, we can see that there are many unnecessary comparisons that are being made.

A possible improvement would be to track not only the smallest unsorted element, but also the largest unsorted element. This would cut down on the number of loops required to go through the list. Since many sorting algorithms are much more efficient, we won't implement this; however, it would be a good exercise to try. It is important to realize that writing programs that simply work is not good enough for the large-scale applications of today.

B. Insertion Sort

In insertion sort, we move through our array starting with the second element, where we place the value in a temporary variable. The value is compared to the elements to the left, one at a time. If the value is larger, then we swap the elements and move to the next element on the left. Otherwise, we move to the next element in our array.

The major improvement of the insertion sort algorithm over selection sort is that once we find an element on the left that is lower than the current value, then we can stop and move on to the next element, since we know that all values before it are already sorted. This lets us stop some of the loops early, which makes our best-case and worst-case values complexities different.

In pseudocode:

```
FOR i FROM 1 TO LENGTH(array) - 1:
  current = array[i]
  j = i - 1
  WHILE j >= 0 AND array[j] > current:
    array[j + 1] = array[j]
    j = j - 1
  array[j + 1] = current
END FOR
```

In the worst case, the array[j] value stays greater than the comparison value until we get back to the beginning of the array. In this case, we would have a time complexity of $O(n^2)$. In the best case, which is an already sorted array, we would exit each loop right away, meaning that we would have a time complexity of $\Omega(n)$. When sorted in place like this, the space complexity is only O(1). The only new data created is the temporary holding variable current.

To further illustrate this, Figure 3.3 shows the sorting of a scrambled array.

Figure 3.3 An example of insertion sort

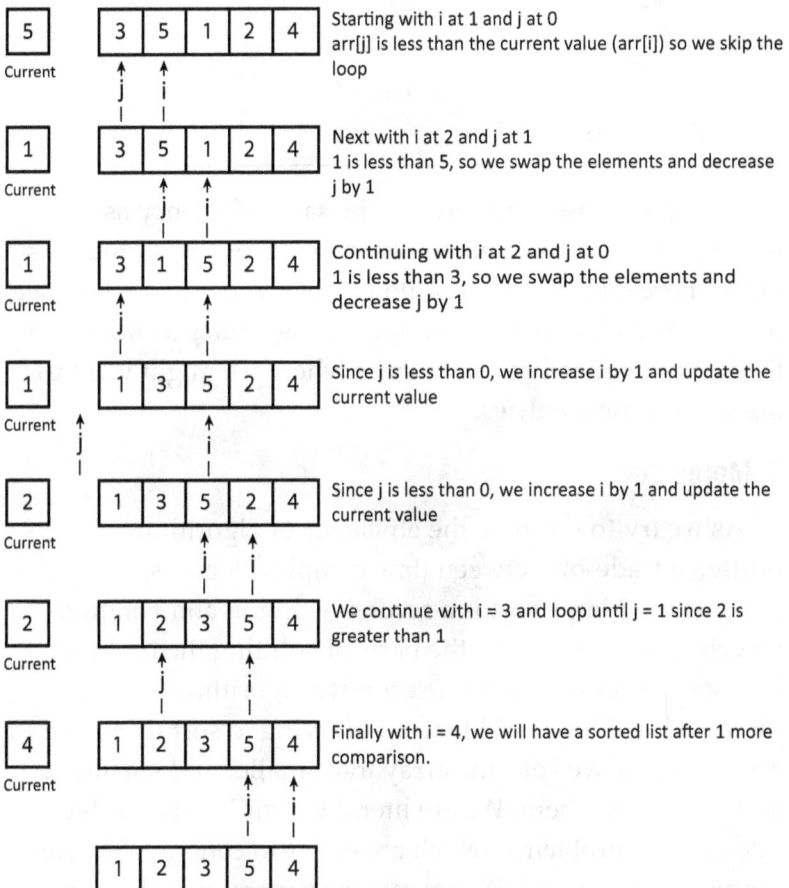

5	3	5	1	2	4	Starting with i at 1 and j at 0
Current						arr[j] is less than the current value (arr[i]) so we skip the loop
	↑j	↑i				

1	3	5	1	2	4	Next with i at 2 and j at 1
Current						1 is less than 5, so we swap the elements and decrease j by 1
	↑j	↑i				

1	3	1	5	2	4	Continuing with i at 2 and j at 0
Current						1 is less than 3, so we swap the elements and decrease j by 1
	↑j		↑i			

1	1	3	5	2	4	Since j is less than 0, we increase i by 1 and update the current value
Current ↑j			↑i			

2	1	3	5	2	4	Since j is less than 0, we increase i by 1 and update the current value
Current						
		↑j	↑i			

2	1	2	3	5	4	We continue with i = 3 and loop until j = 1 since 2 is greater than 1
Current						
	↑j		↑i			

4	1	2	3	5	4	Finally with i = 4, we will have a sorted list after 1 more comparison.
Current						
			↑j	↑i		

	1	2	3	5	4

The implementation in Python is as follows.

```
def insertion_sort(arr):
  for i in range(1, len(arr)):
    current = arr[i]
    j = i - 1
    while j >= 0 and arr[j] > current:
      arr[j + 1] = arr[j]
      j -= 1
    arr[j + 1] = current
  return arr
```

In general, insertion sort has the same efficiency as selection sort. In cases where the array is mostly sorted, it is much more efficient. This could be helpful in cases where we have a sorted list that we are appending values to, such as a list of alphabetized contact names where we might want to insert a few new entries.

C. Merge Sort

As we try to improve the efficiency of algorithms, there is often a trade-off between time complexity and space complexity. Merge sort is a recursive divide-and-conquer algorithm that works on the basis of splitting the problem into smaller subproblems. (Recursive algorithms were discussed in Chapter 2.) Instead of trying to sort the entire array at once, we split the array into smaller and smaller arrays and sort them. We are literally dividing the problem into smaller problems, which are easier to conquer. The new arrays do take up additional memory, increasing the space complexity, but we reuse them when storing the sorted subarrays.

We use two functions to perform a merge sort. The first is used to split the array into two smaller arrays. We recursively do this until we cannot split the array any further. The second function is used to recombine the smaller arrays into sorted arrays until we have all of the elements in order. Splitting the problem into smaller tasks drastically decreases the time complexity.

In pseudocode:

```
FUNCTION merge_sort(array):
    IF LENGTH(array) <= 1:
        RETURN array
    mid = LENGTH(array) // 2
    left = merge_sort(array[0:mid])
    right = merge_sort(array[mid:])
    RETURN merge(left, right)

FUNCTION merge(left, right):
    RESULT = []
        WHILE left AND right:
            IF left[0] <= right[0]:
                APPEND left[0] TO RESULT
                REMOVE left[0]
            ELSE:
                APPEND right[0] TO RESULT
                REMOVE right[0]
        APPEND remaining of left OR right TO RESULT
        RETURN RESULT
```

To split the array apart, we find the middle element using integer division. This returns the result of division rounded down, so splitting an array of length 5 in two will result in an array of length 2 and another of length 3. We continue splitting these split arrays recursively until the arrays are of length 1. Once everything is broken apart, we start at the bottom and sort the smallest arrays, then move up and sort the next set. Since the smaller arrays are already sorted, it makes sorting the larger arrays much simpler. Figure 3.4 shows the process.

Figure 3.4 An example of the `merge_sort()` and `merge()` functions

Breaking down the arrays   Sorting the arrays

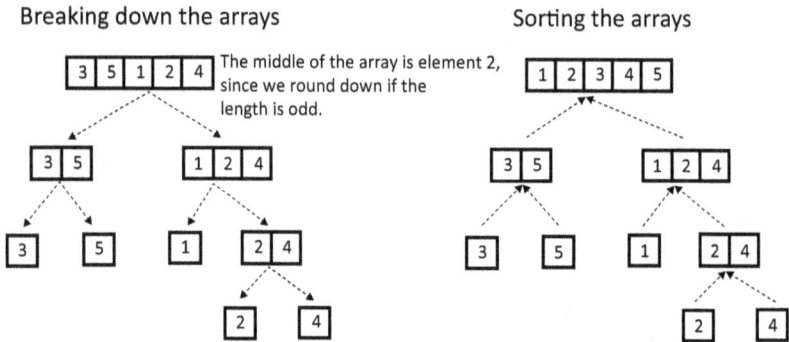

The middle of the array is element 2, since we round down if the length is odd.

The logic for sorting the arrays once they are broken down is fairly simple. We look at the first element in each subarray and place the smaller element into the first index of the array that was broken apart. We then move that pointer to the next element in that subarray and continue the process until the original array is filled. Figure 3.5 shows the sorting of the final array in more detail.

Figure 3.5 Details of the process in the `merge()` function

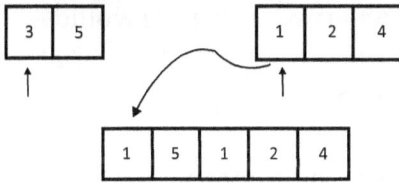

Compare the first two elements, 1 is smaller.
Add the value and increment the index.

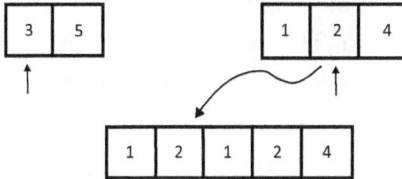

Compare the elements, 2 is smaller.
Add the value and increment the index

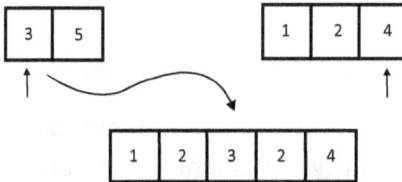

We continue this process until all elements are added to the list.

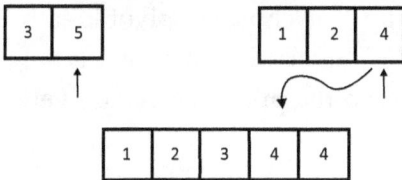

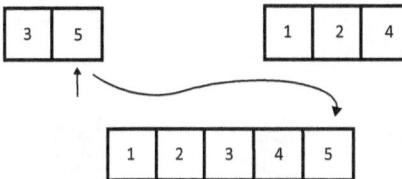

Once the end of one list has been reached,
the remaining elements are added to the list.

In terms of complexity, breaking down the array grows logarithmically with the size of the array. This is due to the repeated division of the array. An array of size 100 would take 7 steps to fully break down, while an array of size 200 would take 8 steps. Sorting and rebuilding the arrays have a linear complexity since each element is being compared during the sort. This makes the overall complexity O(n log n), much better than our earlier attempts. The average and best cases are the same since each step needs to be taken regardless of the nature of the data. The space complexity is O(n) since we are creating arrays for each element in the array during the divide phase. This additional memory cost is more than made up for by the time saved by the algorithm, but there could be cases where memory use is more important than time saved.

D. Quicksort

Another common divide-and-conquer algorithm, which works recursively, is quicksort. A pivot element is selected, and all elements less than the pivot are put into one array and the others into another array. The choice of pivot ideally leads to two roughly equal-sided subarrays. The pivot is placed in the correct locations, and the process is recursively completed with each subarray.

This pseudocode uses the first element as the pivot.

```
FUNCTION quick_sort(array, low, high):
    IF low < high:
        pivot_index = partition(array, low, high)
        quick_sort(array, low, pivot_index - 1)
        quick_sort(array, pivot_index + 1, high)
```

```
FUNCTION partition(array, low, high):
    pivot = array[low]
    i = high + 1
    FOR j FROM high TO low + 1:
        IF array[j] >= pivot:
            i = i -1 1
            SWAP array[i] WITH array[j]
    SWAP array[i -1] WITH array[low]
    RETURN i - 1
```

Again, we use two functions: one for breaking the array down, and one for sorting. There is more than one way to handle quicksort, but this one uses partitioning to cut down on the space complexity. Partitioning is the process of dividing a dataset into groups, in this case, elements that are greater than the pivot and those that are less than or equal to the pivot. This is a little harder to code, but it is much more space-efficient than creating new arrays.

Essentially, we take the first element of the array, in this example, and use that as a reference, called pivot. We use two pointers to move through the data. We start the first index, i, just after the high index and decrement it by one before making any swaps. We start the second index, j, at the high value and compare it to the pivot; if it is greater than or equal, we swap. By the time we make it to the high value, our array is partitioned. Any elements before the pivot will be less than the pivot, and any elements after will be greater than or equal to the pivot. These values are not completely sorted, but are grouped together. The pivot is, however, now at its final resting place. Figure 3.6 illustrates this process.

Figure 3.6 An example of the initial partition call

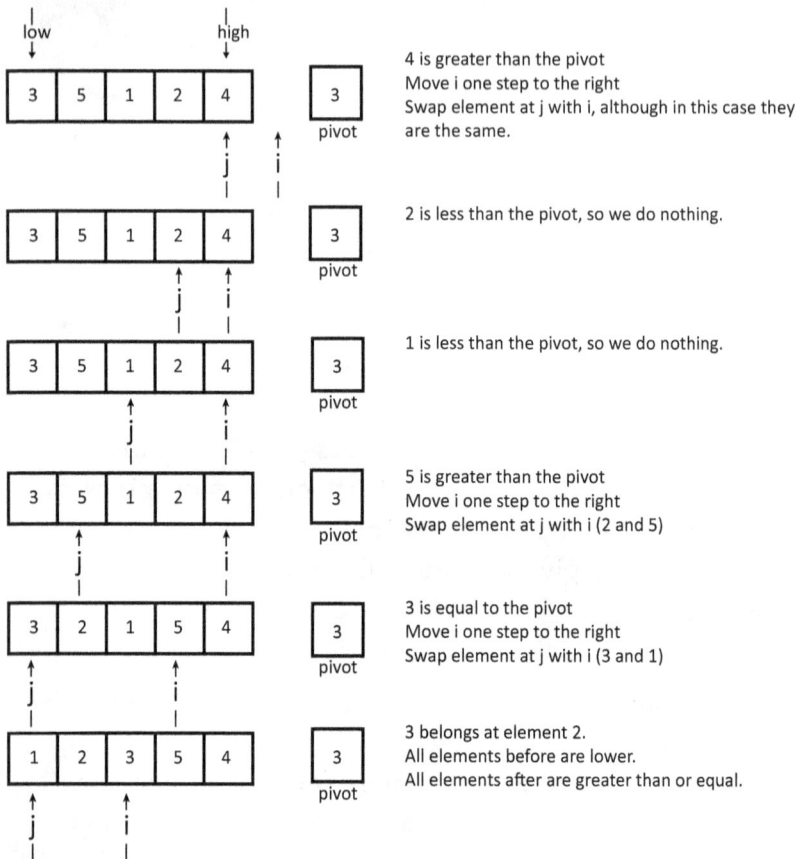

| | | | | | | |
|3|5|1|2|4| |3 pivot|

4 is greater than the pivot
Move i one step to the right
Swap element at j with i, although in this case they are the same.

2 is less than the pivot, so we do nothing.

1 is less than the pivot, so we do nothing.

5 is greater than the pivot
Move i one step to the right
Swap element at j with i (2 and 5)

3 is equal to the pivot
Move i one step to the right
Swap element at j with i (3 and 1)

3 belongs at element 2.
All elements before are lower.
All elements after are greater than or equal.

Once the data is partitioned, the same process is repeated for the part of the data before the pivot and also for the part after the pivot. We continue until each partition is only one element long, which occurs when the low index is no longer less than the high index. Figure 3.7 shows a condensed illustration of this recursive procession, only focusing on the values between low and high indices.

| Figure 3.7 | The recursive nature of the quicksort algorithm |

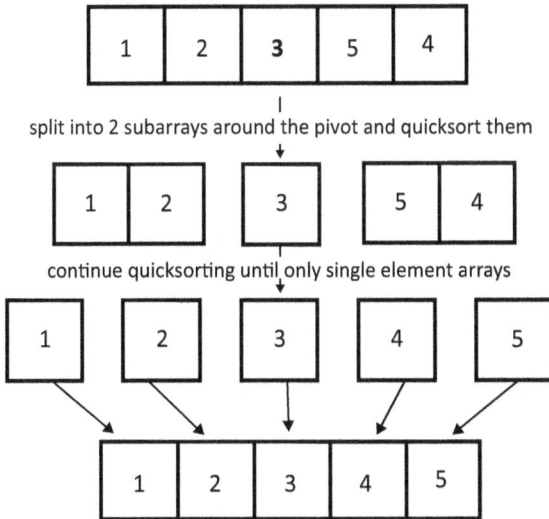

We don't need to recombine the data since we are modifying it in-place. Quicksort has the potential to be, as the name suggests, quick, but this is not always the case. Quicksort functions best when the pivot needs to be placed close to the middle of the data, since this would divide the subarrays into two halves. Unfortunately, if the pivot happens to land near the end of the array, then there wouldn't be much of a reduction in the array size at each level. As designed here with the pivot at the end of the data, this tends to work better for unsorted data than for sorted data.

Incidentally, the Python implementation is:

```python
def quick_sort(arr, low, high):
  if low < high:
    # Partition the array and get the pivot index
    pivot_index = partition(arr, low, high)
    # Recursively sort elements before and after
    # partition
    quick_sort(arr, low, pivot_index - 1)
    quick_sort(arr, pivot_index + 1, high)

def partition(arr, low, high):
  # Choose the last element as the pivot
  pivot = arr[low]
  i = high + 1  # Pointer for the larger element
  for j in range(high, low, -1):
    # Loop backward  through the array
    if arr[j] >= pivot:
      # Compare current element with pivot
      i -= 1
      arr[i], arr[j] = arr[j], arr[i]  # Swap
      # Place the pivot in the correct position
  arr[i -1], arr[low] = arr[low], arr[i -1]
  return i - 1  # Return the pivot index

arr = [3, 5, 1, 2, 4]
quick_sort(arr, 0, len(arr))
print("Sorted Array:", arr)
```

Note that the array name doesn't change since we are modifying it in place. As previously mentioned, this cuts down on the space complexity, but we still have the recursion to deal with. The worst-case complexity is when we have highly unbalanced partitions. In this case, the recursion depth would be the same size as the array, lending to a space complexity of O(n). If the partitions are more balanced, there will be fewer recursions needed, similar to merge sort. This would mean $\Omega(\log n)$ is the best case when partitions are evenly split.

In terms of time complexity, it is closely related to partitions, just as space complexity. In the worst case, we have to loop through everything basically twice, leading to $O(n^2)$; however, if the partitions are even, we perform log n loops, so the best case complexity is $\Omega(n \log n)$.

Table 3.3   Comparison of sorting algorithms

Algorithm	Best Case Time	Average Case Time	Worst Case Time	Space Complexity
Selection Sort	$\Omega(n^2)$	$\Theta(n^2)$	$O(n^2)$	$O(1)$
Insertion Sort	$\Omega(n)$	$\Theta(n^2)$	$O(n^2)$	$O(1)$
Merge Sort	$\Omega(n \log n)$	$\Theta(n \log n)$	$O(n \log n)$	$O(n)$
Quicksort	$\Omega(n \log n)$	$\Theta(n \log n)$	$O(n^2)$	$O(\log n)$

3.3.2 Searching

Having all the data in the world is useless if we can't quickly locate what we are looking for. Searching is one of the most fundamental operations performed on a data structure, and arrays are no exception.

A. Linear Search

Linear search is a brute force algorithm. We start at the beginning and work through the elements until we find what we are looking for. In the best case, we find it quickly, and in the worst case, we find it at the end, or not at all. It should be no surprise that we have $\Omega(1)$ and $O(n)$ based on this description.

Since little new information is being stored, the space complexity is O(1). We just use a simple for loop with a break when the element is found, with the index being returned. Typically, -1 is returned if the element is not found. The benefit of linear search is that the data does not have to be sorted, so it can be used with any data set without any additional operations.

Pseudocode
| ```
FUNCTION linear_search(array, target):
  FOR index FROM 0 TO LENGTH(array) - 1:
    IF array[index] == target:
      RETURN index
  RETURN -1
``` |
| Python implementation |
| ```
def linear_search(arr, target):
  for index, value in enumerate(arr):
    if value == target:
      return index  # Return the index
  return -1  # Return -1 if target not found
``` |

This is such a common algorithm that it's likely anyone reading this book has written a version of it. However, many people don't consider that there might be a more efficient approach.

B. Binary Search

Binary search is a more efficient algorithm, but it requires the data to be sorted for it to work. Binary search works by checking the middle of the data and comparing it to the value we are looking for. If it is not the value, we take half of the data that could be in and search the center of that subset. It may be tempting to approach this as a recursive algorithm, but we've seen how recursion automatically increases space complexity. Instead, we'll use a while-loop to keep the space complexity at O(1).

Pseudocode

```
FUNCTION binary_search(array, target):
  low = 0
  high = LENGTH(array) - 1
  WHILE low <= high:
    mid = (low + high) // 2
    IF array[mid] == target:
      RETURN mid
    ELSE IF array[mid] < target:
      low = mid + 1
    ELSE:
      high = mid - 1
  RETURN -1
```

Python implementation

```
def binary_search(array, target):
  low = 0
  high = len(array) - 1

  while low <= high:
    mid = (low + high) // 2
    if array[mid] == target:
      return mid
    elif array[mid] < target:
      low = mid + 1
    else:
      high = mid - 1

  return -1
```

Much like quicksort, we have two pointers that track the low and high points. The middle value is checked, and if it equals the target value, we return the value of mid. If the middle value is too high, we know the value is in the lower half, so we search between low and mid-1. Otherwise, the value is in the other half, so we search between mid+1 and high. This will often lead us to a quicker result than a linear sort since we halve our search range each time. Figures 3.8 and 3.9 show comparisons of linear search and binary search on sorted data.

Figure 3.8   **Searching for 38 using linear search (7 steps) and binary search (4 steps)**

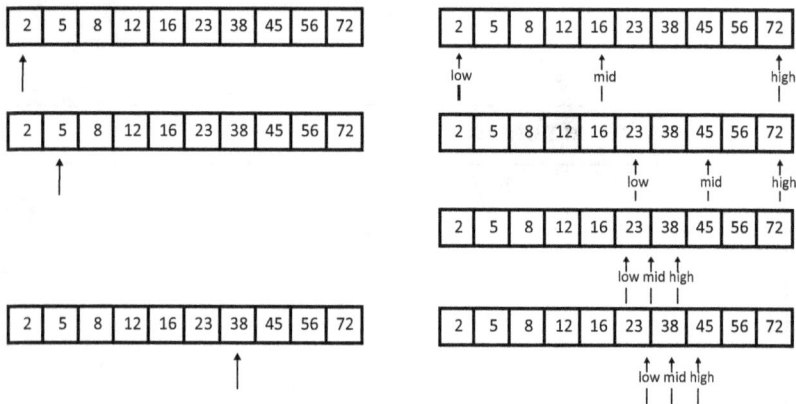

Figure 3.9 Searching for 10 using linear search (10 steps) and binary search (4 steps)

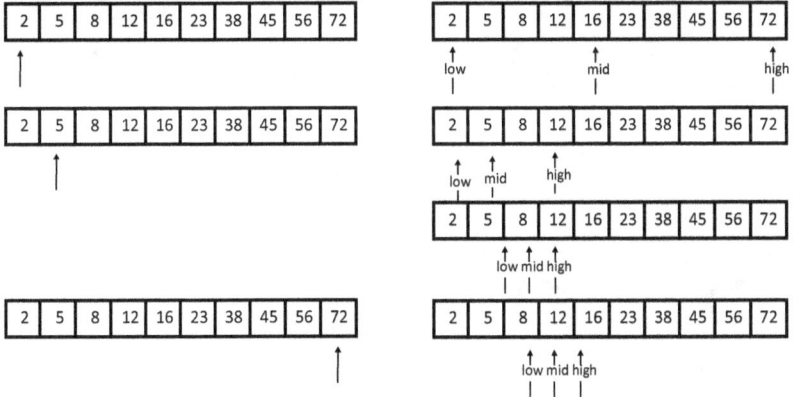

At least for sorted data, binary search tends to be much quicker. Given the previous examples, even if we were searching for 2, the first data point in the set, binary search would only take 3 extra steps over linear search. Figure 3.10 shows just how much time linear search can take compared to binary search for an input of 100 elements.

Figure 3.10 Linear search compared to binary search

Time Complexity of Linear Search and Binary Search

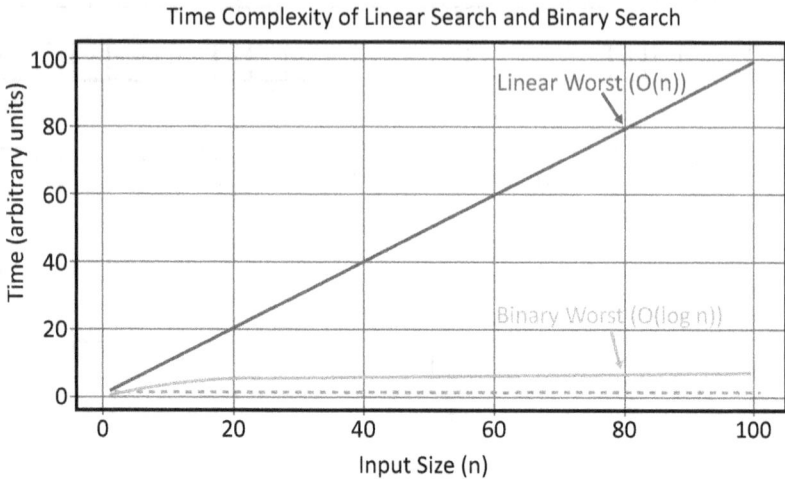

What about unsorted data? Is it worth sorting and then running a binary search, or should we stick to just linear search for such cases? There is no simple answer to this question. Rather, it depends on the specific context of the code.

There are three important factors to consider. First, how large is the dataset? A small, unsorted dataset can typically be searched more quickly using linear search than by sorting it and then applying binary search. The second is the number of searches being performed. If we are looking for multiple items in the array at once, the time lost during sorting is nothing compared to the time we save doing multiple binary searches, especially for large datasets. Third, we need to consider how frequently the data is changing. If the data is constantly in flux, then it would need to be sorted before each search, making the overall process less efficient.

It is important to consider the details of the program we are writing before determining the appropriate algorithm.

This is why we need to understand multiple algorithms, even if they solve the same problem.

3.4   Practical Application – Team Roster

A local Little League team wants a program to help organize their team roster. They have members who join and leave throughout the year, so the roster needs to be updated at various points. Sometimes, they may have delays in their records being updated, so they want to check that they are not adding the same player twice. For convenience, they want to store the names alphabetically. While we worked with numerical values in our examples throughout the chapter, strings can also be searched and sorted by the algorithms that we have already written.

To write this program, we will need functions for adding and removing members, checking if a member is on the team, and sorting the members. We will also add a function to view the team members in alphabetical order.

An array is a great choice to store the data, since we want to be able to sort and search simple data. Since the dataset is small and the list will already be sorted before we add and remove players, insertion sort would work great for this task. For a nearly sorted list, the complexity should be O(n). For searching, linear search is sufficient due to the small dataset, and it's also easier to implement.

```
def insertion_sort(arr):
  for i in range(1, len(arr)):
    current = arr[i]
    j = i - 1
    while j >= 0 and arr[j] > current:
      arr[j + 1] = arr[j]
      j -= 1
      arr[j + 1] = current
      print(arr)
  return arr


def linear_search(arr, target):
  for index, value in enumerate(arr):
    if value == target:
      return index
  return -1
```

The additional functions are then fairly straightforward.

```
def add_member(name):
  index = linear_search(team_roster, name)
  if index == -1:
    team_roster.append(name)
    insertion_sort(team_roster)
  else:
    print(f"{name} is already on the team")


def remove_member(name):
  index = linear_search(team_roster, name)
```

```
if index == -1:
    print(f"{name} is not on the team")
else:
    del team_roster[index]

def print_roster():
    for num, player in enumerate(team_roster):
        print(f"{num+1}: {player}")
```

To add, we find the index using linear search. If the value is not found, we add the new member. Since this operation won't happen frequently, we call insertion_sort() right away. If we were adding several members, it may make more sense not to include this in the function, but to call it later.

To delete, we again find the index and then use the del keyword to remove the name at that index. If the index is -1, the player isn't on the list. Since we are removing the item from the alphabetized list, the remaining items will still be in alphabetical order.

Here is an example usage of our efficient team roster program.

```
team_roster = [
    "Alice", "Bob", "Charlie", "David",
    "Eve", "Frank", "Grace", "Hannah",
    "Isaac", "Jack", "Karen", "Leo",
    "Mona", "Nina", "Oscar"
]

add_member('Jimmy')
remove_member('Eve')
print_roster()
```

Output:

1: Alice

2: Bob

3: Charlie

4: David

5: Frank

6: Grace

7: Hannah

8: Isaac

9: Jack

10: Jimmy

11: Karen

12: Leo

13: Mona

14: Nina

15: Oscar

Chapter Summary

- Arrays store collections of elements, offering efficient data organization and manipulation.

- Python lists act as dynamic arrays (resizable), unlike the static arrays (fixed size) in lower-level languages.

- Insertion, deletion, searching, traversing, and sorting are key array operations.

- Selection sort and insertion sort have higher time complexity, but lower space complexity than merge sort and quicksort.

- Linear search works for unsorted arrays, while binary search is faster for sorted arrays.

- It may be more efficient to sort large arrays to take advantage of binary search's speed.

Quiz

1. **What is the primary characteristic of a static array?**

    a. It can only store integers.
    b. It is always sorted.
    c. It stores data as pointers.
    d. Its size cannot be changed.

2. **Which Python module allows the creation of arrays with specific data types?**

    a. array
    b. collections
    c. list
    d. numpy

3. **In Python, how are lists stored in memory?**

    a. As an array of pointers
    b. As contiguous memory blocks
    c. As individual elements spread across memory
    d. As static memory allocations

4. **Which sorting algorithm is the most efficient for nearly sorted data?**

    a. Selection sort
    b. Insertion sort
    c. Merge sort
    d. Quicksort

5. What is the best-case time complexity of insertion sort?

   a. $\Omega(1)$
   b. $\Omega(n)$
   c. $\Omega(n^2)$
   d. $\Omega(\log n)$

6. Which sorting algorithm divides the array into two halves and recursively sorts them?

   a. Selection sort
   b. Insertion sort
   c. Merge sort
   d. Quicksort

7. What is the space complexity of selection sort?

   a. $O(1)$
   b. $O(n)$
   c. $O(n^2)$
   d. $O(\log n)$

8. What is the space complexity of merge sort?

   a. $O(1)$
   b. $O(n)$
   c. $O(n^2)$
   d. $O(\log n)$

9. In quicksort, what is the pivot used for?

   a. To divide the array into sorted and unsorted parts
   b. To find the middle of the array
   c. To group elements smaller and larger than the pivot
   d. To replace the largest element

10. **What condition must be met for binary search to work?**

    a. The array must be unsorted
    b. The array must be sorted
    c. The array must contain only integers
    d. The array must not contain duplicates

Answer Key

1 – d	2 – a	3 – a	4 – b	5 – b
6 – c	7 – a	8 – b	9 – c	10 – b

CHAPTER 4

Stacks and Queues

Key Learning Objectives

- Understand the Last In, First Out (LIFO) principle of stacks.
- Understand the First In, First Out (FIFO) principle of queues.
- Implement stacks and queues using Python lists and the deque class.
- Explore common stack and queue operations.
- Understand some practical applications of stacks and queues.

In this chapter, we explore stacks and queues. These data structures are fundamental in many algorithms and have practical applications in the real world. Developing a deeper understanding of these structures can help simplify and optimize problem-solving in our code.

4.1 Introduction to Stacks

A stack is a linear data structure that is similar to an array. It follows the Last In, First Out (LIFO) principle. This means that the last element added to the stack is the first one to be removed. We see LIFO in many aspects of our daily lives. When taking a plate out of a cupboard, the one on top was the last one put away. When taking clothes out of a laundry basket, the clothes on the top were the last ones put in. When setting up chairs in an auditorium, the chairs on the top of the stack were the last ones put away.

Figure 4.1   **Stacked chairs illustrating the LIFO principle**

Source: *Photograph by Krišjānis Kazaks. Accessed December 1, 2024.*
https://unsplash.com/photos/rows-of-black-chairs-BH3C4ClTOPY

As a consequence of the LIFO behavior, we can only access the top element at any given time. If we wanted the fifth chair, we would have to remove the first 4 to get to it. Stacks work the same way. There is no traversing or sorting to be concerned with due to this fact. Stacks can also grow and shrink as needed, making lists a great starting point for implementing them in Python. We can use the `append()` and `pop()` methods to quickly create insertion and access.

There is a deque class in the collections that can also model stacks[6]. Deque is short for double-ended queue, which basically means it is a combination of a stack and a queue. This is often the preferred choice in some real-world applications due to its efficiency in some situations. However, in this chapter, we will focus solely on stacks and queues as individual objects. Keep in mind, however, that when dealing with large datasets, deque is a better overall option.

The key operations when working with stacks are `push()` for adding elements and `pop()` for removing and returning the top element. Some other operations that can be useful are `peak()` to check the top element without removing it, `isEmpty()` to ensure there are elements, and `size()` to check the size, although we could just use the `len()` function to do this. When building implementations of data structures, we will be using object-oriented programming (OOP).

Here is the complete implementation with docstrings. All further examples involving stacks will assume that this code has been included in the code or imported as an additional library.

```python
class Stack:
    def __init__(self):
        """
        A basic LIFO (last-in, first-out) stack
        implementation using a list.
        """
        self.stack = []
```

---

6. Python Software Foundation. *"collections — Container Datatypes."* Python 3.12 Documentation. Accessed December 1, 2024. https://docs.python.org/3/library/collections.html.

```python
    def push(self, item):
      """Add an item to the top of the stack."""
      self.stack.append(item)

    def pop(self):
      """
      Remove and return the top item of the stack.
      """
      if not self.is_empty():
        return self.stack.pop()
      else:
        return "Stack is empty"

    def peek(self):
      """
      Return the top item of the stack without
      removing it.
      """
      if not self.is_empty():
        return self.stack[-1]
      else:
        return "Stack is empty"

    def is_empty(self):
      """Check if the stack is empty."""
      return self.size() == 0

    def size(self):
      """Return the size of the stack."""
      return len(self.stack)
```

As can be seen, when we make a new stack, we initialize it with an empty list called stack. push() appends to the stack, while pop() removes and returns from the end of the stack after checking that the stack is not empty. `peak()` is similar to `pop()` without changing the stack. `isEmpty()` checks if the size is zero, while `size()` returns the length of the stack.

Looking at these methods, we can see that none of them depend on the length of the input, and so they all have O(1) time complexity. This makes stacks very efficient data structures.

Once we have our Stack class implemented, we can begin using it.

```
#Create a new stack
stack = Stack()

#Add 10,15,20 to the stack
stack.push(10)
stack.push(15)
stack.push(20)

#Using operations
print(f"Size of the stack is {stack.size()}")
print(f"The top element is {stack.peek()}")
print(f"Popped: {stack.pop()}")
print(f"Popped: {stack.pop()}")
print(f"Is stack empty? {stack.is_empty()}")


Output

Size of the stack is 3
The top element is 20
Popped: 20
Popped: 15
Is stack empty? False
```

4.2 Introduction to Queues

Queues are linear data structures in which only a single element can be accessed at a time. In this way, they are very similar to stacks. The difference is that they follow the First In, First Out (FIFO) principle. The first element to be added is the first to be removed. Line-ups at the grocery store or waiting for the next available agent on a customer service line are real-life examples of FIFO. Queues have all the additional characteristics of stacks.

To implement queues in Python, we use almost the same code, although we name addition as enqueue() and removal as dequeue() instead of push() and pop(). The naming difference here doesn't really matter, but it is a common convention. As with our implementation of stacks, we use object-oriented programming and create a Queue class.

```python
class Queue:
    """
    A basic FIFO (first-in, first-out) queue
    implementation using a list.
    """

    def __init__(self):
        """Initialize an empty queue."""
        self.queue = []

    def enqueue(self, item):
        """Add an item to the rear of the queue."""
        self.queue.append(item)
```

```python
def dequeue(self):
    """
    Remove and return the front item of the
    queue.
    """
    if not self.is_empty():
        # Use the popleft() method
        return self.queue.pop(0)
    else:
        return "Queue is empty"

def peek(self):
    """
    Return the front item without removing it.
    """
    if not self.is_empty():
        return self.queue[0]
    else:
        return "Queue is empty"

def is_empty(self):
    """Check if the queue is empty."""
    return self.size() == 0

def size(self):
    """Return the size of the queue."""
    return len(self.queue)
```

The complexity is very similar to stacks; however, there is one important note about dequeue(). Since we are removing an element from the beginning of the list, the entire list needs to be shifted to the left. This means that we have an O(n) time complexity. This is not a big deal for small queues, but in cases where queues are moderately large, the deque class is a better choice.

Assuming that the Queue class is included in our program, we can create and use queues as shown below.

```
#Create new queue
queue = Queue()

#Add 10,20, and 30 to the queue.
queue.enqueue(10)
queue.enqueue(20)
queue.enqueue(30)

#Using operations
print(f"Front item: {queue.peek()}")
print(f"Dequeued: {queue.dequeue()}")
print(f"Size of queue: {queue.size()}")
print(f"Is queue empty? {queue.is_empty()}")


Output
Front item: 10
Dequeued: 10
Size of queue: 2
Is queue empty? False
```

4.3 Using Deque for Stacks and Queues

4.3.1 Deque for Stacks

There may be times when deque may be more efficient than our previous implementation for stacks. To keep everything working the same regardless of which implementation we use, we can rewrite our Stack class.

Deque has `append()` and `pop()` methods that we can use in place of our list methods. The new implementation is seen below.

```python
from collections import deque

class Stack:
  def __init__(self):
    """
    A basic LIFO (last-in, first-out) stack
    implementation using deque.
    """
    self.stack = deque()

  def push(self, item):
    """Add an item to the top of the stack."""
    self.stack.append(item)

  def pop(self):
    """
    Remove and return the top item of the stack.
    """
    if not self.is_empty():
      return self.stack.pop()
    else:
      return "Stack is empty"

  def peek(self):
    """
    Return the top item of the stack without
    removing it.
    """
```

```
    if not self.is_empty():
      return self.stack[-1]
    else:
      return "Stack is empty"


  def is_empty(self):
    """Check if the stack is empty."""
    return self.size() == 0


  def size(self):
    """Return the size of the stack."""
    return len(self.stack)
```

4.3.2 Deque for Queues

Much like with stacks, we can replace our list with a deque object. Deque has a `popleft()` method that removes the first item in the deque with a complexity of O(1). This allows us to use a queue more efficiently. This is illustrated in the code excerpt below.

```
from collections import deque

class Queue:
  """

  A basic FIFO (first-in, first-out) queue
  implementation using deque.
  """

  def __init__(self):
    """Initialize an empty queue."""
    self.queue = deque()
```

```python
def enqueue(self, item):
    """Add an item to the rear of the queue."""
    self.queue.append(item)

def dequeue(self):
    """
    Remove and return the front item of the
    queue.
    """
    if not self.is_empty():
        # Use the popleft() method
        return self.queue.popleft()
    else:
        return "Queue is empty"

def peek(self):
    """
    Return the front item without removing it.
    """
    if not self.is_empty():
        return self.queue[0]
    else:
        return "Queue is empty"

def is_empty(self):
    """Check if the queue is empty."""
    return self.size() == 0

def size(self):
    """Return the size of the queue."""
    return len(self.queue)
```

Table 4.1 shows the advantages of using deque; however, they are minimal.

Table 4.1	Comparison of complexities between using lists and deque		
Operation	Stacks using Lists	Queues using Lists	Stacks and Queues using deque
Inserting	O(1) amortized	O(1) amortized	O(1)
Accessing	O(1)	O(n)	O(1)
All other operations	O(1)	O(1)	O(1)

We can use either implementation without changing the rest of our code, so the choice depends on the specific project we are working on.

We need to consider whether it is a personal project or something that requires more collaboration. Programmers with experience in other languages may not have access to a library like collections and therefore may prefer to work directly with lists. When studying algorithms for academic or interview purposes, it may be helpful to avoid language-specific ways to cut corners. While certainly useful in programming, overly relying on external libraries may hinder our understanding of basic concepts, or at least give that impression to someone evaluating our skills as programmers.

Implementing data structures manually helps showcase our skills as programmers. Ultimately, regardless of the method we choose, the rest of the code in this chapter will function the same, with little to no difference in overall complexity.

4.4 Stack and Queue-Based Algorithms

Typically, we use stacks and queues to help navigate other data structures, but there are some cases where they can be used to solve problems on their own.

4.4.1 Backtracking

Backtracking is not a single algorithm, but more of an approach to solving problems. Backtracking involves exploring all possible solutions and then undoing parts of those solutions when they fail. It is useful when there are multiple paths or combinations to explore.

In general, we make one decision after another until there are no more to make. If we do not arrive at a correct solution, we undo the last decision and try the next option. If there are no more options for that decision, we undo the previous one and continue this process until all possibilities have been explored or a solution is found.

Backtracking is commonly used for constraint puzzles like Sudoku and solving mazes. It should make sense to use backtracking to solve a maze. We go as far as we can down a given path, and if we hit a dead end, we backtrack the previous step and try again until we find the exit. This is not the most effective method, but it is much better than trying each and every combination.

To solve this backtracking problem, we will use a set to keep track of where we've already been to avoid retrying the same path twice. We will also use a list to hold possible movements, which simplifies our loops. Our maze will be held in a list of lists, commonly referred to as a 2D list. To access a particular point in the 2D list, we use two indices. The first index is the row, or y coordinate, and the second is the column, or x coordinate.

```
maze = [
    [0, 0, 1, 0],
    [1, 0, 1, 0],
    [1, 0, 0, 0],
    [0, 0, 1, 0]
]
```

We will start at maze[0][0], the top left corner, and end at maze[3][3], the bottom right corner. 0s indicate spaces and 1s indicate walls.

```
def solve_maze_dfs(maze, start, goal):
    """
    Solve the maze using backtracking and a stack.
    """
    stack = Stack()
    stack.push(start)
    visited = set()
    visited.add(start)

    directions = [(-1, 0), (1, 0), (0, -1), (0, 1)]
    # Up, Down, Left, Right

    while not stack.is_empty():
        current = stack.peek()
        #Check without removing from stack
        if current == goal:
            # Goal reached, return the path
            return stack.stack

        # Explore neighbors
        valid_neighbor = False
```

```
for dx, dy in directions:
  neighbor = (current[0] + dx, current[1] + dy)
  if (
    0 <= neighbor[0] < len(maze) and
    0 <= neighbor[1] < len(maze[0]) and
    neighbor not in visited and
    maze[neighbor[0]][neighbor[1]] == 0
  ):
    stack.push(neighbor)
    visited.add(neighbor)
    valid_neighbor = True
    break
if not valid_neighbor:
  # If no valid neighbors, backtrack
  stack.pop()

# If no path found
return None
```

In our code, we initialize our stack and add our starting position to both the stack and the visited set. Next, we check all of the squares around the start for a valid place to move. Once all valid positions are added to the stack and the visited set, we move to the last added square and repeat the process, remembering that previously added squares to the visited set are not valid. This pushes us through the maze until we hit a dead end. Popping additional elements off the stack will take us down other paths that we did not explore. This continues until we either reach the goal or run out of options in the stack. The process is sometimes called depth-first search, or DFS, since we are going all the way to the end of a particular path before searching another. Figure 4.2 shows the process in more detail.

Figure 4.2   Navigating a 2D maze with a stack

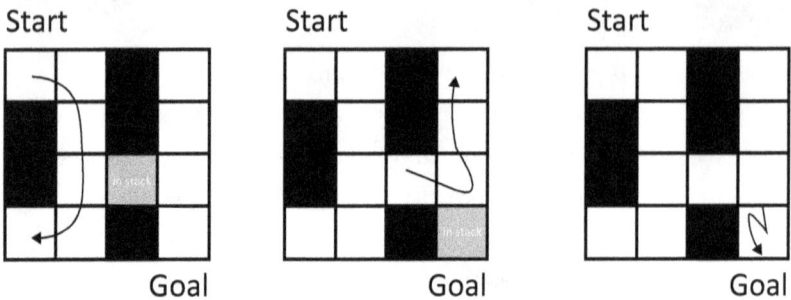

The worst-case time complexity of the maze algorithm for a square maze is $O(n^2)$, where n is the size of the maze; however, we tend to write it as $O(R \times C)$ since the rows and columns would be different for a rectangular maze. This is due to the fact that each cell in the maze would need to be processed if there is no path out of the maze. The space complexity is also $O(n^2)$ for a square maze, or $O(R \times C)$ in general, since all cells may need to be added to our visited set or stack. This is acceptable for small to moderate-sized mazes, but larger mazes do require more advanced algorithms to be solved efficiently.

While not a backtracking approach, we can also use queues to solve the maze. The main benefit is that the queue method will not just find a path to the end, but it will find the shortest path. This is true for our example maze, though it may not always be the case in more complex scenarios. However, as with most things, there are trade-offs. Since we are no longer maintaining a stack that includes our movements, we need to store the path for every possibility we might explore. This increases the space complexity since we could be storing multiple long paths.

Using queues uses a breadth-first search, or BFS. Unlike DFS, BFS checks all options at one level before moving to the next. In terms of our maze, we determine every position we could end up at after 1 step, check if one is the goal, and then check every position after 2 steps. This continues until we hit the goal or run out of possible steps.

Figure 4.3 shows the squares being checked at each level to illustrate the process of using a queue.

Figure 4.3 The squares search at each level of the BFS search using queues

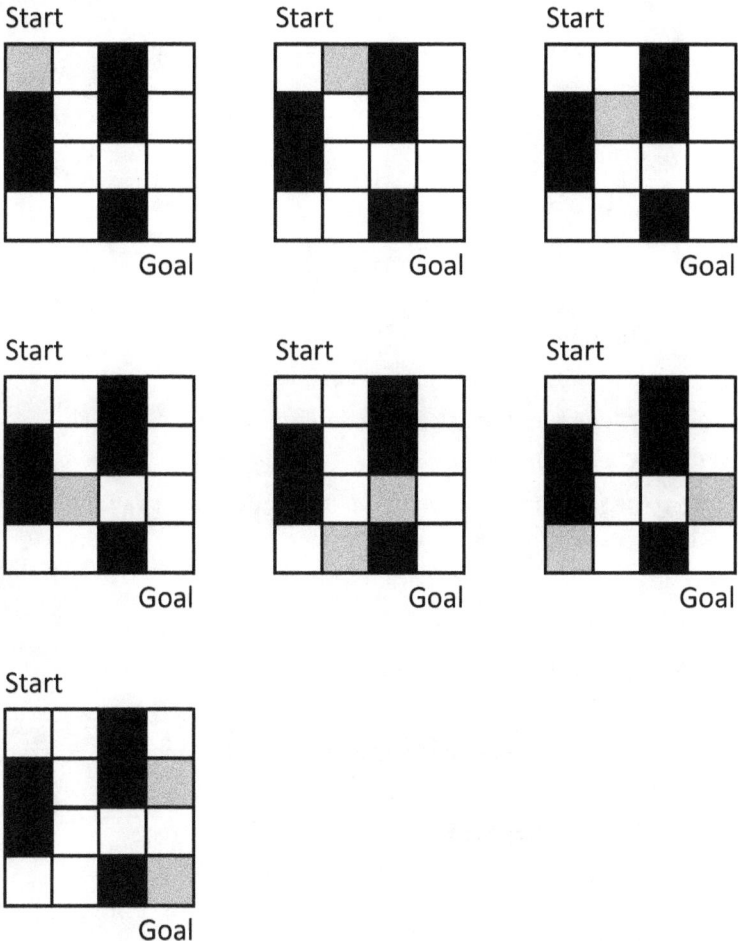

The code to implement this algorithm is similar to the stack version. The main differences are that we need to store the path to each square, and that we use dequeue to remove from the front of the queue instead of pop to remove from the end of the stack.

```
def solve_maze_bfs(maze, start, goal):
    """Solve a maze using a queue."""
    queue = Queue()
    # Queue to store cells to explore
    queue.enqueue((start, [start]))
    # Each item is (current_position, path)
    visited = set()
    visited.add(start)

    directions = [(-1, 0), (1, 0), (0, -1), (0, 1)]
    # Up, Down, Left, Right

    while queue:
        current, path = queue.dequeue()
        # Dequeue the front element
        if current == goal:
            # Return the path if the goal is reached
            return path

        for dx, dy in directions:
            neighbor = (current[0] + dx, current[1] + dy)
            if (
                0 <= neighbor[0] < len(maze) and
                0 <= neighbor[1] < len(maze[0]) and
                neighbor not in visited and
                maze[neighbor[0]][neighbor[1]] == 0
            ):
```

```
queue.enqueue(
    (neighbor, path + [neighbor])
)
# Add neighbor to the queue
visited.add(neighbor)


# If no path is found
return None
```

The time complexity of this algorithm is also O(n²) for square grids or O(R × C) for rectangular ones. This is because we may have to search through each cell to find an exit, or determine that none exists. The space complexity has the potential to be much higher since we are storing not only the queue of space and visited information, but also the path to each queued location. For square grids, this is a complexity of O(n²) or O(R × C) for non-rectangular grids. This makes it very memory-intensive for larger grids.

4.4.2 Balanced Parentheses Problem

When we write code, we need to make sure that each opening parenthesis has a matching closing parenthesis. Using stacks, we can write an algorithm to ensure that this is the case. The main idea of this algorithm is to first ignore anything that is not a parenthesis.

Second, we need to store any opening parenthesis that we see into a stack. When we find a closing parenthesis, we will pop() the latest value off the stack to ensure it matches. We will use a dictionary to store which opening and closing parentheses are paired. If all values have a match and the stack is empty at the end of the algorithm, we know there are no unpaired parentheses.

```
def is_balanced(s):
  stack = Stack()
  bracket_map = {")":"(", "]":"[","}":"{"}
  for char in s:
    #if the character is an open parenthesis,
    # push it to the stack
    if char in bracket_map.values():
      stack.push(char)
    #if the character is a closing parenthesis,
    # check the stack
    elif char in bracket_map.keys():
      if (
        stack.is_empty()
        or stack.pop() != bracket_map[char]
      ):
        #if the stack is empty or
        # the wrong character is on top
        return False
  return stack.is_empty()
```

Figure 4.4 shows how the string (3x[2-1]) can be verified using our algorithm.

Figure 4.4 Using stacks to solve a balanced parenthesis problem

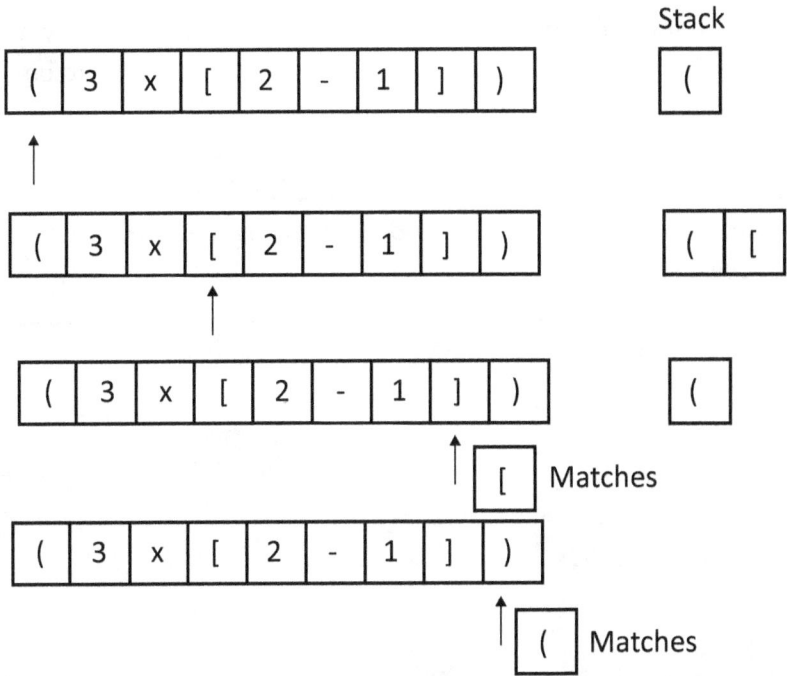

The time complexity for this algorithm is O(n), where n is the length of the string, since we need to loop through the whole string once. The worst-case space complexity is O(n) since the stack could potentially grow to the size of the list.

4.5 Practical Applications – Browser History and Print Queues

4.5.1 Browser History

Consider a company that is developing a web browser for a new mobile device. They want to ensure that users can easily navigate to previously visited web pages. They want an efficient way to manage this, especially since the device will have limited memory.

To handle this task, we would likely use a stack. This way, we'll always have the most recently visited page ready to be retrieved. Whenever the user visits a new page, the page is pushed to the stack. When the back button is pressed, the last page is popped off the stack and loaded. Assuming we also include our Stack class, the code for adding and retrieving pages is rather straightforward.

```python
def visit_page(current_page, new_page):
    """Visit a new page"""
    #If already on a page, put in on the stack
    if current_page:
        history.push(current_page)
    print(f"Visited: {new_page}")
    return new_page


def go_back(current_page):
    """Navigate to previous page"""
    #Go back if there is a page to go back to
    if history.size() > 0:
        previous_page = history.pop()
        print(f"Back to: {previous_page}")
        return previous_page
    #Other stay on the same page
    else:
        print("No pages in history")
        return current_page
```

```
history = Stack()
current_page = None

current_page = visit_page(
   current_page, "https://docs.python.org/"
)
current_page = visit_page(
   current_page, "https://www.python.org/"
)
current_page = visit_page(
   current_page,
   "https://www.vibrantpublishers.com/"
)
# Back to https://www.python.org/
current_page = go_back(current_page)
# Back to https://www.gutenberg.org/
current_page = go_back(current_page)
# No pages in history
current_page = go_back(current_page)
```

This allows us to quickly and efficiently store and retrieve visited websites using the Stack class, which we previously implemented.

4.5.2 Print Jobs

Managing print jobs is a great application of queues, as we want the first job sent to be the first job printed. Using the First-In, First-Out (FIFO) principle ensures fairness to the print queue. To implement an example of this, we can use our Queue class created earlier.

```python
# Instantiate the print queue
print_queue = Queue()

def add_job(job_name):
    """Add a new print job to the queue."""
    print_queue.enqueue(job_name)
    print(f"Added job: {job_name}")

def process_job():
    """Process the next print job in the queue."""
    if not print_queue.is_empty():
        job = print_queue.dequeue()
        print(f"Processing job: {job}")
    else:
        print("No jobs in the queue.")

# Example Usage
add_job("Document1.pdf")
add_job("Report.docx")
process_job()
add_job("Photo.jpg")
process_job()
process_job()
process_job()

Output

Added job: Document1.pdf
Added job: Report.docx
Processing job: Document1.pdf
```

```
Added job: Photo.jpg
Processing job: Report.docx
Processing job: Photo.jpg
No jobs in the queue.
```

In the example, we can see that even though the report was added after the document, the report still prints first. The use of queues not only makes the program efficient, but it also makes the code compact and readable.

Stacks and queues are versatile tools that assist programmers in solving problems related to order, navigation, and efficient data management. As we tackle more complex challenges, remember that even simple structures can serve as the foundation for intricate algorithms. By mastering these fundamental tools, we lay the groundwork for designing elegant and efficient solutions.

Chapter Summary

- Stacks are linear data structures that follow the Last In, First Out (LIFO) principle.

- Queues are linear data structures that follow the First In, First Out (FIFO) principle.

- Stacks and queues can be implemented through lists or using the deque class in the collections library.

- Depth-First Search (DFS) can be implemented with stacks to fully explore a path to its endpoint before backtracking to explore alternative solutions.

- Breadth-First Search (BFS) can be implemented with queues to explore all adjacent elements at the current level before proceeding to elements at the next level.

Quiz

1. **Which operation is used to add elements to a stack?**
   a. enqueue()
   b. peek()
   c. pop()
   d. push()

2. **What is the time complexity of the** push() **operation?**
   a. O(1)
   b. O(n)
   c. O(log n)
   d. O(n²)

3. **Which method is used to view the top element of a stack without removing it?**
   a. dequeue()
   b. enqueue()
   c. peek()
   d. pop()

4. **Which principle are queues based on?**
   a. First In, First Out
   b. First In, Last Out
   c. First Out, First In
   d. First Out, Last Out

5. **Which operation removes an element from a queue?**
   a. dequeue()
   b. enqueue()
   c. pop()
   d. push()

6. **What is the main drawback of using lists to implement queues in Python?**

   a. Removing an element requires shifting the remaining elements

   b. They are immutable

   c. They cannot store heterogeneous data

   d. They do not support FIFO

7. **What does deque stand for?**

   a. Double Efficient Queue

   b. Double-Ended Queue

   c. Dynamical Enhanced Queue

   d. Data Enriched Queue

8. **What is the benefit of using deque over a list for creating queues?**

   a. deque allows O(1) insertion and removal from both ends

   b. deque automatically sorts elements

   c. deque is immutable

   d. deque supports multiple data types

9. **What is backtracking?**

   a. A method to iterate through all possibilities and undo choices when necessary

   b. A method to solve problems by sorting elements

   c. A way of minimizing time complexity

   d. A way to optimize memory usage

10. What is the main data structure used in backtracking?
    a. Dictionary
    b. List
    c. Queue
    d. Stack

Answer Key

1 – d	2 – a	3 – c	4 – a	5 – a
6 – a	7 – b	8 – a	9 – a	10 – d

CHAPTER 5
Linked Lists

Key Learning Objectives

- Understand the differences between singly and doubly linked lists.
- Perform linked list operations such as insertion, deletion, traversal, and reversal.
- Analyze the time and space complexity of linked list operations.
- Explore key algorithms and real-world applications.

In this chapter, we explore linked lists, a dynamic data structure that provides an efficient way to store and manipulate data. Unlike arrays, linked lists allow for flexible memory allocation, making them useful when data needs to grow or shrink dynamically. We will examine the different types of linked lists and their applications.

5.1 Introduction to Linked Lists

Linked lists, as the name suggests, are lists of data that are linked together. Unlike arrays, linked lists do not store elements in contiguous memory locations but instead store a reference to the location of the next linked element. It's a bit like a treasure hunt where we receive information about the next location as we continue along the path.

Figure 5.1	Treasure map: An analogy for linked lists

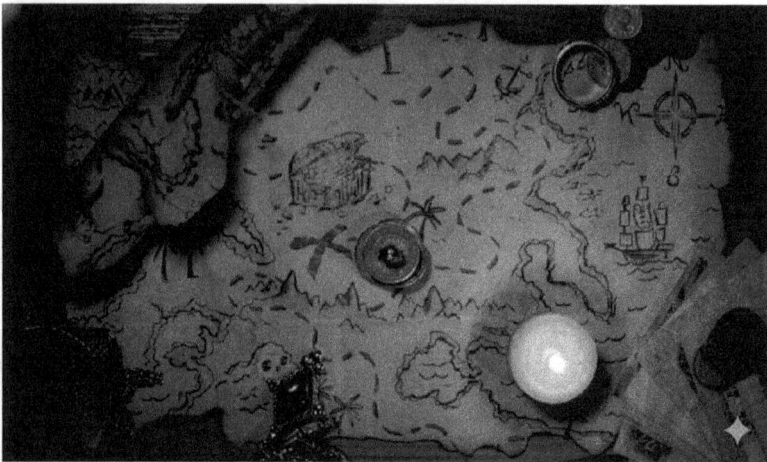

Source: Photograph by Nadjib BR.
https://unsplash.com/photos/brown-and-beige-ceiling-lamp-51Ms-0PbCHo

The elements that make up a linked list are known as nodes. Each node contains two parts: the data and a pointer to the next node. The first node is known as the head and is the starting point of operations for the linked list. The final node is sometimes referred to as the tail.

Since the location of the next item is always known, we can add and remove items from a linked list without worrying about the memory allocation needing to be changed. This may not seem like a major issue, however, in applications where data changes frequently, there is considerable time lost in shifting array items around.

Consider a scenario where we are deleting the second element of a ten-item array. We would need to shift all of the remaining items down one index. What if the array were a hundred elements or thousands? Linked lists do not have this problem, as we simply need to update the pointer that used to point at the removed node to point at the next node. Regardless of the length of the linked list, only one pointer needs to be updated. Figure 5.2 shows this process in more detail.

Figure 5.2 Deleting an item from a list compared to a linked list

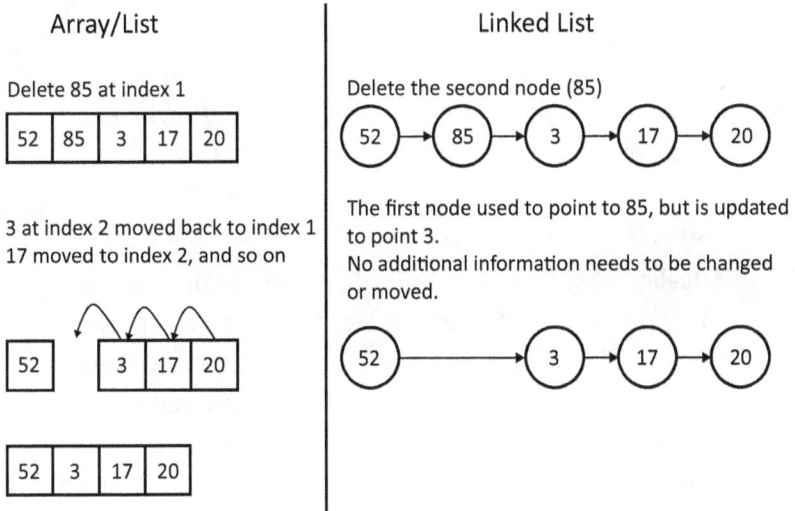

Array/List

Delete 85 at index 1

| 52 | 85 | 3 | 17 | 20 |

3 at index 2 moved back to index 1
17 moved to index 2, and so on

| 52 | | 3 | 17 | 20 |

| 52 | 3 | 17 | 20 |

Linked List

Delete the second node (85)

52 → 85 → 3 → 17 → 20

The first node used to point to 85, but is updated to point 3.
No additional information needs to be changed or moved.

52 ──────→ 3 → 17 → 20

The major trade-off is that we no longer have an index to reference values. All traversals have to start at the head of the linked list and continue along the path from there. This means that many of the array-based algorithms that we learned about in Chapter 2 will not work for linked lists. Also, while the concept of linked lists is fairly straightforward, the implementation and utilization of them can be a little trickier. Learning linked lists is well worth the challenge, as they are a great starting point for learning about pointers and have many practical uses.

5.2 Types of Linked Lists

There are several types of linked lists, but all of them work under the same general idea of nodes storing data and pointers to the next node. The simplest form we've already seen: the singly linked list. When we say a linked list, we normally mean a singly linked list.

A. **Singly linked lists:** These lists start with a head node and end with a node that points to None. They can only be traversed in one direction as a node only contains information about the next node, not the previous one. If we wish to go back to a previous node, we need to start over from the head again. This is the obvious disadvantage of a singly linked list, but they are simpler to implement and they use less memory.

B. **Doubly linked lists:** A list of this type contains all the same information as a singly linked list, but also contains a reference to the previous node. If we need to travel in both directions, a doubly linked list can make some operations more efficient, however, they are more complex to implement and require more memory to store the additional pointers.

Circular linked lists can also be used, in which the last node points back to the head. These can be singly or doubly linked and have some specific use cases, such as circular queues, but they will not be a focus in this text.

When choosing whether to use a singly or doubly linked list, it is important to consider the problem that we are trying to solve. For example, if we were navigating through a music playlist, we may want to be able to move forward or backward, so a doubly linked list would be useful. If we wanted software to store and read maintenance logs, a singly linked list would do, as we would normally want to access them in a forward sequence.

5.3 Linked List Operations

To start developing linked lists, we need to consider the operations required, such as inserting, deleting, and traversing. We will specifically work with singly linked lists as their implementation is simpler. As with previous data structures, we will be using object-oriented programming. We will also use a separate class for our nodes and our linked links.

Typically, we would just call the node class *Node*; however, to separate our singly and doubly linked lists, we will call it *SinglyNode*. It will be created with the data and an empty pointer. This is because we will not have created the next node to pass it in. We will assign the pointer after. We do want to assign self.next to None to avoid any attribute errors.

```
class SinglyNode:
    """A node in a singly linked list."""
    def __init__(self, data):
        self.data = data
        self.next = None
```

Our singly linked lists will start empty and be built up by nodes later. We start by assigning the head to None, again to avoid attribute errors.

```
class SinglyLinkedList:
  """A simple singly linked list implementation."""
  def __init__(self):
    self.head = None
```

5.3.1 Traversal

Traversing through linked lists always starts at the head. We use a temporary variable to check the track of the *current* node. If the node has a value for the *next* attribute, then we know there is another entry in the linked list. We reassign the *current* node to this *next* node and continue until there is no next node. Since we loop through the entire list, the time complexity is O(n).

```
def traverse(self):
    """Print the contents of the list."""
    current = self.head
    while current:
      print(current.data, end=" -> ")
      current = current.next
    print("None")
```

Typically, we wouldn't need to traverse the linked list on its own. However, this method can be useful for printing out the entire list. The logic behind the traversal is important for inserting and deleting information into the linked list.

5.3.2 Insertion

To start adding to our linked list, we will need more than one method. To start, we will have a method for adding to the beginning and another for adding to the end. When we insert at the beginning, the data being inserted will become the new head of the linked list, and the current head will be pointed to by the new head. Everything else remains the same, so the method is fairly simple.

```
def insert_at_beginning(self, data):
    """Insert a node at the beginning of the list."""
    new_node = SinglyNode(data)
    new_node.next = self.head
    self.head = new_node
```

First, we create a new node with the data. Next, we take the current head of the list and assign it to the new node's next attribute. Finally, we assign the new node to the head of the list. This has O(1) time complexity since it does not vary based on the length of the linked list.

Adding to the end of the linked list is a little trickier because we don't have any way of directly accessing the tail. Instead, we have to start at the head and continue accessing the next nodes until we reach a node with no next node. Once we have the last node, we assign the new node as its next node.

```
def insert_at_end(self, data):
    """Insert a node at the end of the list."""
    new_node = SinglyNode(data)
    if not self.head:
        self.head = new_node
        return
    current = self.head
    while current.next:
        current = current.next
    current.next = new_node
```

Here we make the new node as before, then check to see if the value of `self.head` is not None. In the case where the linked list is empty, we insert the new node as the head. Next, we use the variable *current* to mark our location in the list, starting with the head. We check if there is a next node, and if there is, we assign it to *current*. Once we find a node without a next node, we know we are at the end. We assign our new node to the next node of *current*. Since we need to navigate through the entire linked list to do this, we have a time complexity of O(n).

We can modify our `insert_at_end` method to insert at a particular position as well. Since linked lists don't have indices, we need to start at the head and move the desired number of nodes before inserting. The added trouble is that we will need to update two pointers. We also have to be sure the position is valid.

To implement this, we first make sure that we are passing in a position that is greater than zero. We then create the new node and traverse through the linked list until we hit the intended position, keeping track of the previous node as we go. If we hit the end of the list before reaching the position, then the position is out of bounds. To handle out-of-bounds conditions, we will raise a ValueError.

Assuming we have a valid position, the previous node will need to point to our new node, and our new node will point to the next node of the previous node. Figure 5.3 shows this process in more detail.

Figure 5.3 Inserting a value into a given position in a linked list

Inserting 18 at position 2

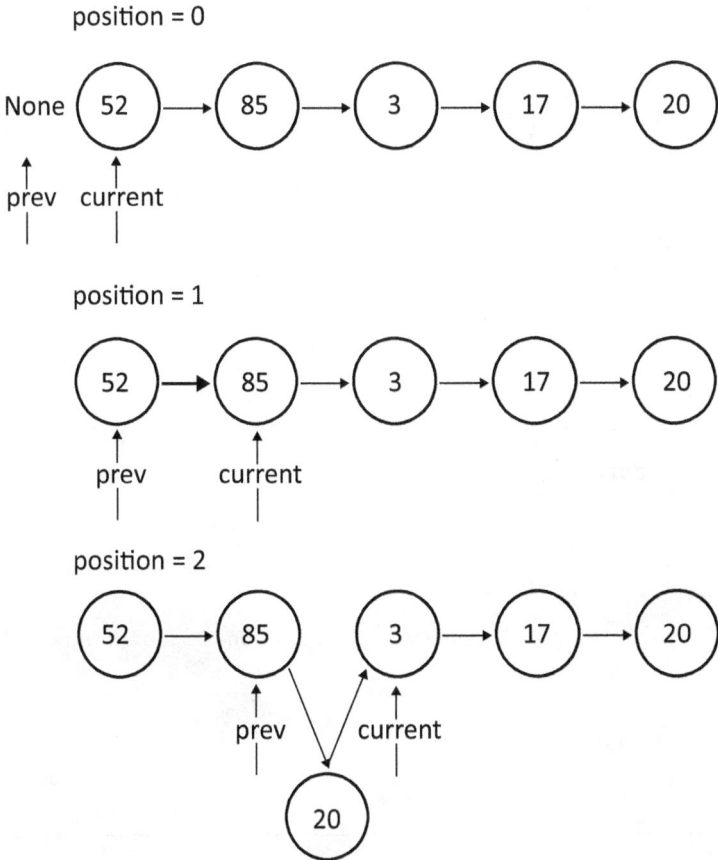

position = 0

None (52) → (85) → (3) → (17) → (20)

prev   current

position = 1

(52) → (85) → (3) → (17) → (20)

prev   current

position = 2

(52) → (85)   (3) → (17) → (20)

prev   current

(20)

In code form, we have:

```python
def insert_at_position(self, position, data):
    """
    Insert a node at a specific position in the list.
    """
    if position < 0:
        raise ValueError(
            "Position must be a non-negative integer."
        )
    new_node = SinglyNode(data)
    if position == 0:
        new_node.next = self.head
        self.head = new_node
        return
    current = self.head
    prev = None
    for _ in range(position):
        if not current:
            raise ValueError("Position out of bounds.")
        prev = current
        current = current.next
    new_node.next = current
    prev.next = new_node
```

5.3.3 Deletion

Deletion involves removing a node and updating the pointers. Much like with insertion, we can do so from the beginning, end, or at a specific position, but for simplicity, we will just write a single function to take a position to delete. We can also search for a specific value and delete the appropriate node.

If we want to delete based on a position, we traverse the linked list until we find the specific position, keeping track of both the current and previous nodes. Once we find the node at the correct position, we take its next node and connect it to the previous node. Since there are no more references to the node we want to remove, Python's garbage collection will remove it from memory. Much like with insertion, we will also need to raise errors if we are outside of the allowed bounds. In essence, the only real difference is that instead of changing pointers to a new node, we are connecting the previous node to the next node of the removed node.

```python
def delete_at_position(self, position):
    """
    Delete the node at a specific position
    in the list.
    """
    if position < 0:
        raise ValueError(
            "Position must be a non-negative integer."
        )
    current = self.head
    if position == 0:
        if current:
            self.head = current.next
        return
    prev = None
    for _ in range(position):
        if not current:
            raise ValueError("Position out of bounds.")
        prev = current
```

```
    current = current.next
if not current:
    raise ValueError("Position out of bounds.")
prev.next = current.next
```

Deleting by value follows the same logic, however, we use a while loop to move through the list until we find the specific value.

```python
def delete_node(self, key):
    """
    Delete the first node with the given
    data value.
    """
    current = self.head
    if current and current.data == key:
        self.head = current.next
        return
    prev = None
    while current and current.data != key:
        prev = current
        current = current.next
    if current is None:
        return
    prev.next = current.next
```

5.3.4 Doubly Linked Lists

When it comes to doubly linked lists, our nodes must have both a next and a previous attribute.

```
class DoublyNode:
  """A node in a doubly linked list."""
  def __init__(self, data):
    self.data = data
    self.next = None
    self.previous = None
```

The doubly linked list class initializes the same as for a singly linked list, but will also include a tail attribute. This is optional, but it allows us to traverse from the end of the list more efficiently. Some singly linked lists also use a tail pointer for applications where we might want to start at the end, such as implementing a queue structure from a linked list.

```
class DoublyLinkedList:
  """
  A doubly linked list supporting bidirectional
  traversal.
  """
  def __init__(self):
    self.head = None
    self.tail = None
```

The basic implementation of the methods will remain mainly the same. However, whenever inserting, we will need to update two pointers: the next and the previous. Fortunately, since each node contains a next and previous attribute, we no longer need to track these with temporary variables. This approach makes the code more elegant, but it does require more memory for all of the assigned references.

```python
def insert_at_beginning(self, data):
    """
    Insert a node at the beginning of the list.
    """
    new_node = DoublyNode(data)
    new_node.next = self.head
    if self.head is not None:
        self.head.prev = new_node
    else:
        self.tail = new_node
        # If inserting into an empty list,
        # update tail
    self.head = new_node

def insert_at_end(self, data):
    """Insert a node at the end of the list."""
    new_node = DoublyNode(data)
    if self.head is None:
        self.head = self.tail = new_node
        return
    self.tail.next = new_node
    new_node.prev = self.tail
    self.tail = new_node

def insert_at_position(self, position, data):
    """
    Insert a node at a specific position in the
    list.
    """
    if position < 0:
        raise ValueError(
            "Position must be a non-negative integer."
        )
```

```
new_node = DoublyNode(data)
if position == 0:
  self.insert_at_beginning(data)
  return
current = self.head
for _ in range(position - 1):
  if not current:
    raise ValueError("Position out of bounds.")
  current = current.next
new_node.next = current.next
if current.next:
  current.next.prev = new_node
else:
  # Update tail if inserting at the end
  self.tail = new_node
new_node.prev = current
current.next = new_node
```

Likewise, deletion follows the same pattern, with some additional logic to update the tail if necessary.

```
def delete_by_value(self, value):
    """
    Delete the first node with the given value
    """
    current = self.head
    while current:
      if current.data == value:
        if current.prev:
          current.prev.next = current.next
```

```
        else:
          # Update head if first node is deleted
          self.head = current.next
        if current.next:
          current.next.prev = current.prev
        else:
          # Update tail if last node is deleted
          self.tail = current.prev
        return
      current = current.next
    raise ValueError("Value not found in list.")


  def delete_by_position(self, position):
    """
    Delete a node at a specific position in the
    list.
    """
    if position < 0:
      raise ValueError(
        "Position must be a non-negative integer."
        )
    current = self.head
    if position == 0:
      if current:
        self.head = current.next
        if self.head:
          self.head.prev = None
        else:
          self.tail = None  # List is now empty
        return
    for _ in range(position):
```

```
        if not current:
            raise ValueError("Position out of bounds.")
            current = current.next
        if not current:
            raise ValueError("Position out of bounds.")
        if current.prev:
            current.prev.next = current.next
        if current.next:
            current.next.prev = current.prev
        else:
            # Update tail if deleting last node
            self.tail = current.prev
```

Unlike singly linked lists, traversal is possible in both directions with a doubly linked list. With a tail pointer, we can start from the last node and traverse back toward the head. The logic of traversing from the head until there is no next node is duplicated in reverse, starting from the tail until there is no previous node.

```
    def traverse_forward(self):
        current = self.head
        while current:
            print(current.data, end=" <-> ")
            current = current.next
        print("None")
```

```
def traverse_backward(self):
    # Start from the tail instead of traversing
    # first
    current = self.tail
    while current:
        print(current.data, end=" <-> ")
        current = current.prev
    print("None")
```

Doubly linked lists offer more flexibility but are more complex and require additional memory. Table 5.1 compares singly and doubly linked lists.

Table 5.1   Comparing singly and doubly linked lists

Feature	Singly Linked List	Doubly Linked List
Memory Usage	Requires less memory due to only having one pointer.	Requires more memory due to having two pointers.
Insertion / Deletion	Efficient at head, but slows with traversal.	Efficient at both head and tail.
Traversal	Forward only.	Forward and backward.
Complexity	Simpler to implement.	More complex due to the additional pointer.
Use Cases	Stacks, lists, and queues.	Navigation, undo / redo functions.

5.4   Linked List-Based Algorithms

5.4.1 Floyd's Tortoise and Hare

Linked lists can be a challenging data structure. Either on purpose, such as creating a circular linked list, or by accident, such as assigning an incorrect node, we can create a cycle within our linked list. Attempting to traverse a linked list that cycles could create memory problems and possibly an infinite loop.

In thinking about this problem, it might be tempting to create an array to track visited nodes, and while these brute force ideas would work, they would not be very efficient. First, the space complexity would be O(n) since we would be storing new information about each node. Time complexity would also be fairly high due to having to traverse through the entire linked list, but also having to compare the current node to the items stored in the array. This would lead to a time complexity of O(n²) since, ultimately, we would need to compare the last item to an array containing potentially the entire linked list. With both high space and time complexity, this approach is not acceptable.

To detect a cycle efficiently, we use two pointers: a slow pointer and a fast pointer - often referred to whimsically as the tortoise and the hare. The logic here is that if there is an end to the linked list then the hare should quickly reach it; however, if there is a loop in the path, the hare will eventually cross paths with the tortoise again. In our implementation, the hare will move two steps at a time while the tortoise moves one. Figures 5.4 and 5.5 show this idea in more detail.

Figure 5.4 An illustration of Floyd's Tortoise and Hare without a cycle

Both pointers start at the head

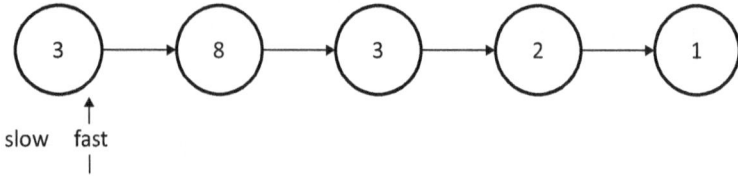

slow   fast

Fast moves two nodes, while slow only moves one

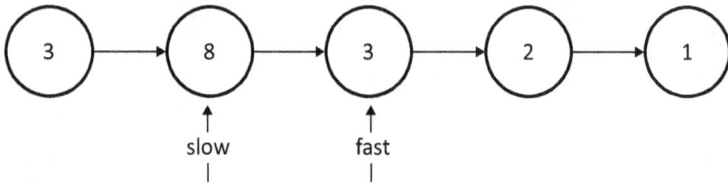

slow   fast

Since fast eventually points at a node with no next in two steps there is no cycle. Making two steps at a time makes this faster than traversing one at a time.

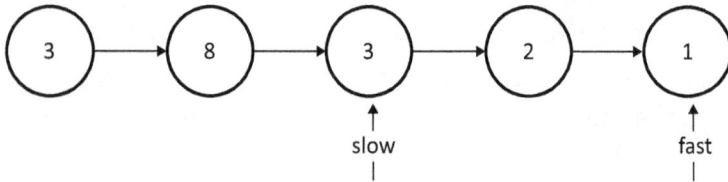

slow   fast

Figure 5.5 An illustration of Floyd's Tortoise and Hare with a cycle

Both pointers start at the head and more as normal

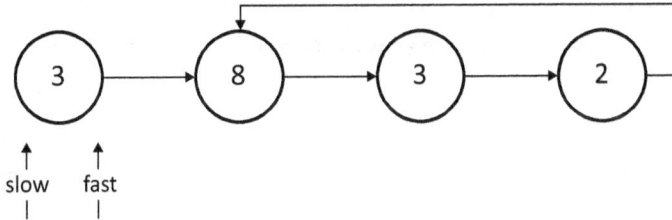

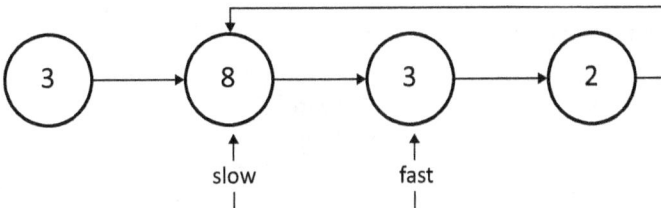

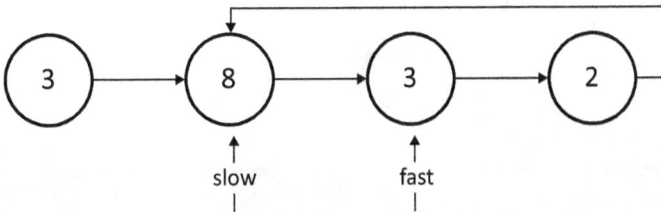

Since both pointers end up at the same place before an end is found, we know there is a cycle.

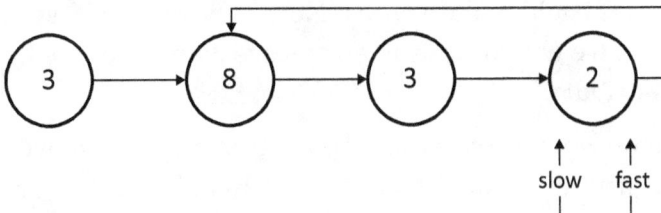

To implement the algorithm, we will use our singly node and singly linked list classes. The method detect_cycle() can be written into our singly linked list class. We set both slow and fast to the head of the list and then start

traversing the list. Slow moves one step at a time, while fast moves two steps. If we used larger steps for fast, we could prove that a list didn't cycle by reaching the end quicker, but we might miss the tortoise and have to make multiple passes, leading to a larger worst-case time complexity. We continue looping until we find no next for the fast pointer, meaning there is no cycle, or slow equals fast, meaning there is a cycle.

The method is as shown.

```
def detect_cycle(self):
    slow = fast = self.head
    while fast and fast.next:
        slow = slow.next
        fast = fast.next.next
        if slow == fast:
            return True
    return False
```

By checking that both fast and fast.next are not None, we can safely ensure that we are at the end of the list. If we tried to simply check fast.next.next without verifying that fast.next exists, we could end up with a NoneType error. If fast.next is None, we would raise an error since None does not have a next attribute.

In the worst case, the slow pointer manages to move through all the nodes before being caught by the hare, so we have a time complexity of O(n), although on average it would perform much better. The space complexity is O(1) since only the new slow and fast pointers are created, regardless of the input size. This algorithm nicely illustrates the usage of pointers and highlights a simple solution to a problem that could seem quite challenging at first.

5.4.2 Finding the Middle of a Linked List

Since linked lists do not use indexing, it is more difficult to find the middle of a linked list. We also do not typically store the length of the linked list, so it is not as simple as counting in a set number of nodes.

As a brute force attempt, we may try to first get the length by traversing the list, then divide by two to get the central node, and traverse to that point. This however, would require us to navigate through the list one and a half times, making it inefficient. Temporarily storing nodes to allow us to recall the middle node without going back through would require a fair amount of extra space.

The efficient path would be to use a slow and fast pointer, like in Floyd's tortoise and hare. If the fast pointer travels twice as fast as the slow pointer, then it should reach the end of the list in half the time as the slow pointer. To reframe this, the slow pointer will be halfway through the list by the time the fast pointer gets to the end. Our algorithm will move the slow and fast pointers until the fast pointer reaches the end and then we will return the slow pointer.

```
def find_middle(self):
  slow = fast = self.head
  while fast and fast.next:
    slow = slow.next
    fast = fast.next.next
  # Slow pointer now points to the middle node
  return slow
```

The time complexity is O(n) since we go through the list once and the space complexity is O(1) since the pointers do not change based on the length of the list. Finding the middle of a linked list can be helpful for implementing sorting and searching algorithms as we did with arrays, or checking a linked list for symmetry, such as palindrome checking, a common interview question.

5.4.3 Reversing a Linked List

We have seen that when it comes to singly linked lists we have to traverse from the head to the end of the list. This is fine when dealing with operations that flow in that direction, but if we need to flow in reverse, this would be a problem. True, doubly linked lists would solve this issue, but there can be times when the added memory needs to be avoided. Rewriting the linked list in the reverse order would allow us to traverse in the opposite direction, and if we overwrite the original list it doesn't need to take up more memory. The question is how to do this efficiently.

To reverse a list we have no choice but to traverse through the entire list and have the current node point to the previous node. Once the end of the list is reached, we will assign the last value as the head. We have a choice to implement this iteratively or recursively, but both have a time complexity of O(n) as the whole list has to be traversed. Both will be implemented as methods to our singly linked list class. There is not much point to reverse a doubly linked list, since it can be traversed in reverse anyway, however a simple method could be implemented where we swap previous and next.

The iterative approach involves storing the previous node and the next node in temporary variables. This allows us to update the next node to the previous while still having the ability to move to the next node in our original sequence.

We also have an optional starting node. This will allow us to reverse a part of a list which will come in handy later in the chapter.

```
def reverse_linked_list(self, start_node=None):
  prev = None
  current = start_node or self.head
  while current:
    next_node = current.next
    current.next = prev  # Reverse the pointer
    prev = current
    current = next_node
  self.head = prev
```

Since the linked list is modified in place there are only the temporary variables which take up additional space. Since these do not depend on the length of the list, we have a constant time complexity, O(1).

The recursive method requires a base case which here will be when there are no more next nodes or if a node itself is None. We recursively pass in the next node and continue until the base case. Once the base case is hit, the list is reversed piece by piece.

```
def reverse_recursive(self, node):
    # Base case: If node is the last node or None,
    # return it as the new head
    if not node or not node.next:
        self.head = node
        return node
```

```
# Recursively reverse the rest of the list
reversed = self.reverse_recursive(node.next)

# Make the next node point back to the
# current node
node.next.next = node
# Set current node's next to None to avoid cycles
node.next = None

return reversed
```

Like all recursive methods, this suffers from increased space complexity. The function call stack grows in relation to the length of the input linked list, so the space complexity is linear, or O(n). Since the recursive version is more space complex, has the same time complexity, and really doesn't offer any benefits in terms of implementation. The iterative version is the clear winner in this case.

5.5 Practical Application - Palindrome Checking

A palindrome is a sequence that reads the same forward and backward, ignoring spaces and punctuation. Simple examples include "Taco cat" and "Madam I'm Adam", but there are countless others. We could approach this problem with doubly linked lists, but the extra memory use is not ideal. Instead, we will find the middle node of our list and reverse the second half. We can traverse with two pointers from the middle node, one moving toward the head, and one moving toward the end of the reversed section. If it is a palindrome, we should have the same values at each step. We stop when we find two nodes with different values or if the second list runs out of elements. In the event that the phrase has an odd number of characters the first list will have the extra central character which can be ignored since it would be compared with itself. Figure 5.6 shows the process in detail.

Figure 5.6 Checking for palindromes

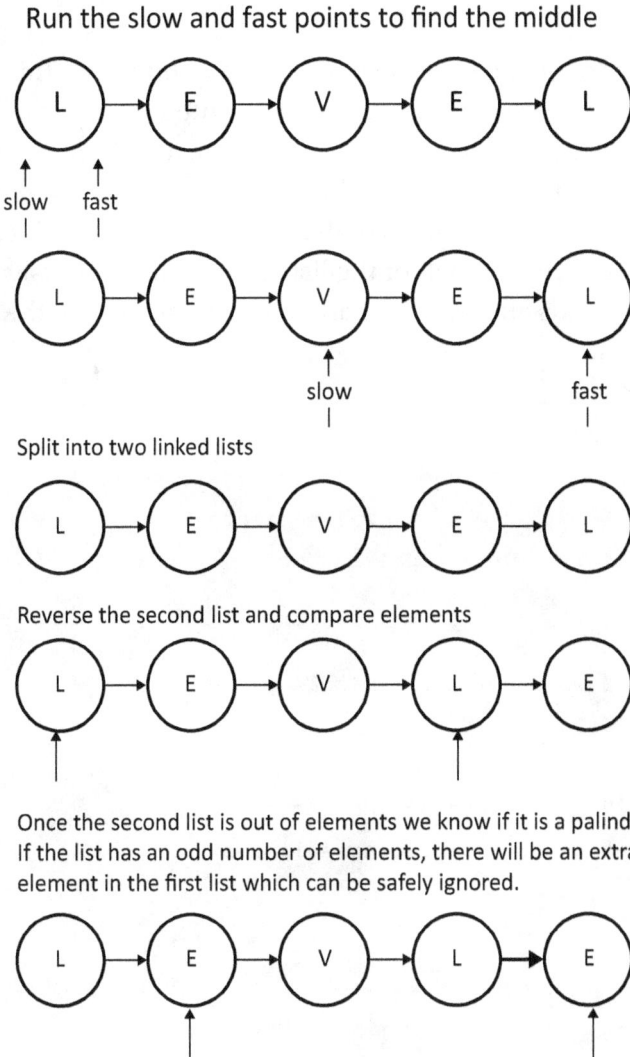

Run the slow and fast points to find the middle

Split into two linked lists

Reverse the second list and compare elements

Once the second list is out of elements we know if it is a palindrome. If the list has an odd number of elements, there will be an extra central element in the first list which can be safely ignored.

We should also consider some edge cases where we have
an empty linked list, or one that only contains one node.
We will consider an empty linked list to be a palindrome
since it is hard to consider emptiness as asymmetrical.
Likewise, a linked list containing only a single node will also
be considered a palindrome. We can return True for both
of these cases without having to go through the rest of the
algorithm.

We have actually done most of the heavy lifting for this
algorithm since we have our class along with methods to
find the middle and reverse a list. Using the iterative version
of our list reversal and passing in the node after the middle
node will cut down on the overall amount of traversal since
we are only reversing half of the list. Using our previously
written methods allows us to only focus on the logic of the
comparison.

```
def is_palindrome(self):
    if not self.head or not self.head.next:
        # A list with 0 or 1 elements
        # is always a palindrome
        return True

    # Step 1: Find the middle of the list
    middle = self.find_middle()

    # Step 2: Reverse the second half
    reversed = self.reverse_linked_list(middle)
```

```
# Step 3: Compare both halves
left, right = self.head, reversed
# Only need to compare half the list
while right:
  if left.data != right.data:
    return False
  left = left.next
  right = right.next

return True
```

While there are multiple operations with linear time complexity, since each one runs in linear time, we consider the total time complexity to be O(n). The space complexity is O(1) since again we are not creating any new lists, just a few temporary variables.

Linked lists provide a powerful and flexible way to work with data. They are essential when working with dynamic data as we can use them to insert, delete, and traverse new data without having to worry about large memory overhead. Linked lists are also used with other data types to create even more versatility.

Chapter Summary

- Linked lists store collections of elements dynamically which allows for efficient insertions and deletions, without memory reallocation.

- Singly linked lists allow forward traversal, while doubly linked lists allow for traversal forward and backward.

- Slow and fast pointers can be used to detect cycles and find the middle node of a linked list.

- Linked lists offer advantages in situations where frequent modifications are required.

- Linked lists lack direct indexing, so they are not useful in many situations.

Quiz

1. **What is a key advantage of using linked lists over arrays?**
   a. Constant time indexing
   b. Dynamic memory allocation
   c. Faster traversal speed
   d. Fixed memory allocation

2. **In a singly linked list, what does each node contain?**
   a. Data and a pointer to the next node
   b. Data and a pointer to the previous node
   c. Data only
   d. A pointer to the previous node and a pointer to the next node

3. **Which linked list operation has an average time complexity of O(1)?**
   a. Deleting the last node in a singly linked list
   b. Inserting a node at the beginning
   c. Searching for a node
   d. Traversing the entire list

4. **How does Floyd's Tortoise and Hare algorithm detect a cycle in a linked list?**
   a. By maintaining a hash table of visited nodes
   b. By reversing the linked list and checking for duplicates
   c. By using a single pointer that moves through the list
   d. By using two pointers moving at different speeds

5. **In a doubly linked list, what does each node contain?**

   a. Data and a pointer to the next node

   b. Data and a pointer to the previous node

   c. Data and two pointers: one to the previous node and one to the next node

   d. Data only

6. **What is the time complexity of reversing a singly linked list iteratively?**

   a. $O(1)$

   b. $O(\log n)$

   c. $O(n)$

   d. $O(n^2)$

7. **What is a key advantage of a doubly linked list over a singly linked list?**

   a. Has constant-time deletion anywhere in the list

   b. Requires less memory

   c. Supports bidirectional traversal

   d. Uses fewer pointers

8. **What is the best way to insert a new node at the end of a singly linked list?**

   a. Perform a binary search to find the last node

   b. Reverse the list and insert at the beginning

   c. Traverse the entire list to the last node and update its next pointer

   d. Use a tail pointer to track the last node

9. What is the time complexity of searching for a value in an unsorted linked list?

   a. O(1)
   b. O(log n)
   c. O(n)
   d. O(n²)

10. What is the primary reason why linked lists use more memory than arrays?

   a. Each node stores additional pointer references.
   b. They must store metadata about their length.
   c. They require contiguous memory allocation.
   d. They require frequent memory reallocation.

Answer Key

1 – b	2 – a	3 – b	4 – d	5 – c
6 – c	7 – c	8 – d	9 – c	10 – a

CHAPTER 6

Hash Tables

Key Learning Objectives

- Understand the fundamentals of hash tables, such as keys, hash functions, and collision handling.
- Implement chaining and open addressing to handle collisions.
- Explore different hashing methods such as modular hashing, mid-square hashing, and multiplicative hashing.
- Apply hash tables to real-world situations.

In this chapter we will explore hash tables, a powerful data structure that provides an efficient way to store and retrieve data. Unlike arrays and linked lists, hash tables have extremely efficient lookups, insertions, and deletions, making them ideal for many tasks.

6.1   Introduction to Hashing

We've seen in past chapters that sorting and searching through data can take a lot of time, memory, or both. If we could find a way to efficiently determine where information would be stored without searching through the data structure, it would save a lot of time. This is where the hash table comes in.

6.1.1 Hash Table Basics

Hash tables provide efficient lookups, insertions, and deletions by calculating where data should be stored within the table. A hash function is used to compute the index, or hash code, where the data should be stored in the array-like structure. Hash tables often use key-value pairs, with the key being used with the hash function to determine the index where the value will be placed. To keep the examples simple to start, we will use a single data point for both the key and value.

There are many hash functions, but the simplest method is modulo hashing. Modulo hashing involves taking the key and getting the modulo of it with the size of the table. For example, if we wanted to put the value 35 in a hash table of size 10, we would do:

35 % 10 = 5

So 35 would go into bin 5. This would be the equivalent of index 5 if we were building our implementation off of a list structure.

In general, a good hash function must satisfy several properties. First, it should be quick to calculate. Second, it should always give the same output for a given key. Finally, it should create a well-distributed set of indices. This helps avoid collisions – an extremely important concept which we will explore shortly.

We will be using modulo hashing for all examples, unless otherwise specified.

The size of the table to be used is also an important factor to be considered. If we have 5 keys to store and we use a table with 5 bins there is a very high chance that some of the values will have the same hash value, meaning they will try to occupy the same bin. At the same time, using a table with 50 bins would lead to having a lot of wasted space. In general, a smaller table can save memory, but performance can be affected due to more collisions needing to be resolved. A larger table requires more memory, but performs better since there are fewer collisions.

For now, we will use a hash table twice the size of our data set but we can often get away with having a smaller table. In real applications, we would try to keep the ratio of data to table size under 0.7. This ratio is called the load factor. Mathematically, this would make our table size 1.42 times our data size, but for simplicity we will just double it.

If we wanted to place the values 13, 25, 47, 59, and 70 into a hash table, it would be reasonable to use a table with 10 bins. Table 6.1 shows how the values would be placed into a 10-bin hash table.

Table 6.1 Determining the hash codes for a data set

Value	Hash Code (Value % 10)	Bin
13	13 % 10 = 3	3
25	25 % 10 = 5	5
47	45 % 10 = 7	7
59	59 % 10 = 9	9
70	70 % 10 = 0	0

70			13		25		47		59

If we wanted to see if the value 52 was in our hash table, we would calculate the hash code (52 % 10 = 2) and check to see if it is in bin 2. Since the bin is empty, we know that 52 is not in our table. It can be a little more complex if a different value is in the bin, but we'll discuss that when we talk about handling collisions.

This works well for integer data, but float data would give decimal value bin numbers, and strings would give errors, since the modulus operator cannot be applied to strings. There are a few ways that this can be dealt with, such as rounding floats or converting strings to the sum of their ASCII values, but Python provides a simple function, hash(), not to be confused with a hash function.

Values determined by hash() are the same during the current runtime of a Python execution, but will vary due to a random value set by Python at the moment of execution, so the values produced during a second runtime will be different. The important thing is that they are the same during the same execution to avoid expected results. This randomness is done to allow for a better average time complexity.[7] Table 6.2 shows some keys and their hash() values during a particular Python execution.

7. Python Software Foundation, "Data Model," Python 3 Documentation, Accessed December 13, 2024, https://docs.python.org/3/reference/datamodel.html#object.__hash__.

Table 6.2	Keys and their hashed keys determined using `hash()`	
Key	Hashed Key	Hash Code (into 8 bins)
5	5	5
"Tomato"	8356459216270398292	4
"tomato"	7584407702065809124	4
"Newfoundland"	-428150268484112518	2

We could then calculate hash codes for these hashed keys and set up a hash table. Unfortunately, we would have two keys to place into bin 4.

6.1.2 Collision Basics

A. Chaining

When two keys have the same hash value, we end up with a collision. This creates a problem since both keys cannot be placed in the same bin. Collisions in hash tables are inevitable, so we need to know how to handle them. There are two main methods of handling collisions: chaining and open addressing.

The easiest to understand and implement is chaining. To chain, we use a linked list as our bin and create a chain of values that go in the bin. This simple method can handle multiple collisions at the target index, but uses additional memory for the linked list.

Figure 6.1 uses chaining to store the values 23, 44, 31, 85, and 93 in a 10 bin table.

| Figure 6.1 | Placing values into a hash table of size 10 using chaining |

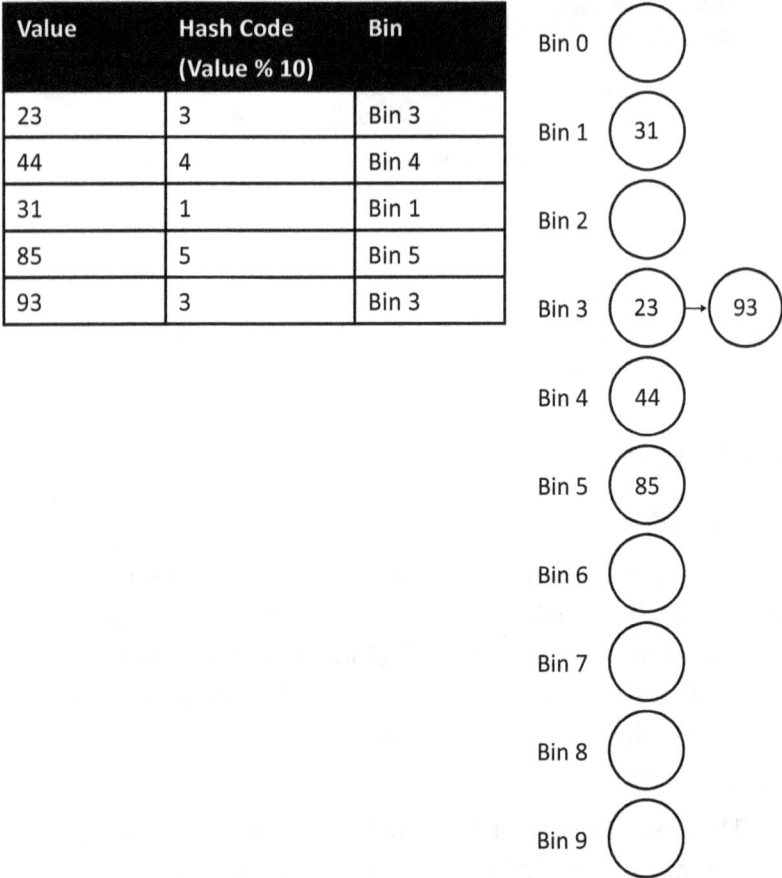

Value	Hash Code (Value % 10)	Bin
23	3	Bin 3
44	4	Bin 4
31	1	Bin 1
85	5	Bin 5
93	3	Bin 3

Bin 0

Bin 1 — 31

Bin 2

Bin 3 — 23 → 93

Bin 4 — 44

Bin 5 — 85

Bin 6

Bin 7

Bin 8

Bin 9

Now, if we wanted to verify that 93 was in the table, we would check bin 3 and traverse the linked list until we either find 93 or hit the end of the linked list. It takes more time to traverse the list, but if the table is a sensible size and the hash function spreads out the data, none of the linked lists should be overly long.

On average, operations involving chained hash tables have a time complexity of O(1) since most chains should be short, ideally one element. The worst case would be if all the elements ended up in a single chain. At that point, we would need to work our way through the entire chain, giving a complexity of O(n). This can be avoided by using a good hash function and a large enough table.

Deleting items in a chained table is similar in nature to deleting an item in a linked list, which we learnt in the previous chapter. This has an average complexity of O(1) since the item will likely be found at the beginning of the list.

B. Open Addressing

The main alternative to chaining is open addressing. Open addressing uses a probing sequence to find an empty bin when a collision occurs. It is common to use a linear probe, meaning we move one bin at a time until we find an empty bin. Other probes will be discussed later.

If we store the values 23, 44, 31, 85, and 93, this time using open addressing, we end up placing 93 in bin 6 as it is the next available bin, as seen in Table 6.3.

Table 6.3	Placing values into a hash table of size 10 using open addressing		
Value	Hash Code (Value % 10)	Desired Bin	Bin to be Used
23	3	Bin 3	Bin 3
44	4	Bin 4	Bin 4
31	1	Bin 1	Bin 1
85	5	Bin 5	Bin 5
93	3	Bin 3	Bin 6

To locate a value, such as 105, we calculate the hash code (105 % 10 = 5), which leads us to bin 5. We find 85 there, so we continue with our linear probe. Bin 6 contains 93, and bin 7 is empty, so 105 is not in the table. This method avoids the extra memory of storing linked lists, however, there can be more time involved in searching, especially when the table grows fuller.

The average case for operations would also be O(1), since ideally there will be no collisions and no probing will be required. In the worst case, when the table is full or the data is clustered, the table could need to be fully scanned to complete operations. In this case, the complexity would be O(n).

Deleting items when using open addressing is quite a challenge, since deleting an element would break the probing sequence.

Considering our previous example:

	31		23	44	85	93			

If we wanted to delete 85, we would first calculate its hash code, which would be 5 (85 % 10). Since 85 is located in bin 5, it can be deleted. If that were the only step, then looking up any values that previously collided with 85 would no longer be found. Looking up 93, for example, would result in a hash code of 3 (93 % 10). Bins 3 and 4 are occupied, but not by 93. Bin 5 is now empty, so the algorithm stops looking, never finding 93 in bin 6.

	31		23	44		93			

To prevent this behavior, we have to add a marker to indicate that a value has been removed. This special marker will be indicated by the value "DELETED". This will allow us to replace it when adding new values and also pass over it when looking up values.

	31		23	44	DELETED	93			

As the number of markers increases, the performance for looking up values decreases since the table becomes fuller. It has no impact on insertion. Deleting itself, like insertion, has an average time complexity of O(1) and a worst case of O(n).

Both chaining and open addressing provide efficient ways to handle collisions in hash tables. This ensures that data remains accessible regardless of the number of identical hash values. To minimize the extra time needed to handle collisions, we can also look at methods of minimizing collisions.

6.2 Probing Methods and Hash Functions

6.2.1 Probing Methods

When dealing with collisions in open-addressing, we have a choice in how to find the next appropriate bin number. We used linear probing in our earlier examples. Using a linear probe where we simply checked the next bin one after the other until we found an empty bin. This is a simple method, but it tends to result in clustered values. Since this can lead to increases in probing lengths, let us discuss some other methods.

A. Quadratic Probing:

To avoid clustering, quadratic probing can also be used. Quadratic probing checks 1 bin away, then 4 bins away, 9 bins away, and so on. The modulus operation is used to wrap the values around if we move past the end of the bins. The formula new_index = (hash_index + i ** 2) % table_size

can be used to determine the next bin to probe. Figure 6.2 shows the process of assigning the values 23,33,43, and 53 using quadratic probing.

Figure 6.2 **Using quadratic probing**

23 should be placed in bin 3 (23% 10 = 3)

			23						

33 should be placed in bin 3 (33% 10 = 3)
Since it is full, we check bin 4 ($3 + 1^2$), which is empty

			23	33					

43 should be placed in bin 3 (43% 10 = 3)
Since it is full, we check bin 4 ($3 + 1^2$), which is also full.
Next we check bin 7 ($3 + 2^2$), which is empty.

			23	33			43		

If we wanted to place 53, we would end up using bin 1, since bin 3, 4, and 7 are already used.
$3 + 3^2 = 11$
11% 10 = 1

	53		23	33			43		

We have to be careful with quadratic probing, as we can end up looping back to the same values and miss some of the empty spaces. To avoid this problem, the hash table should have a prime number length and should be resized if it starts to become full. Resizing, however, is no easy task as it involves rehashing all of the values already in the table.

Quadratic probing does minimize clustering at first, but can lead to secondary clustering. This is due to the fact that the sequence for avoiding clustering follows the same sequence.

B. Double Hashing:

Another method of probing is known as double hashing. In the event of a collision, we calculate a new step size for checking bins. If designed well, this method should not loop and should ensure a good distribution of data. The formula

step = prime - key % prime

gives the step size to use in the event of a collision, where prime is the next prime number lower than the table size. One benefit of this method is that each colliding value could potentially have a different step size, meaning that there may not be additional collisions. Figure 6.3 shows this process, using 7 as the prime number.

Figure 6.3 Probing with double hashing

23 should be placed in bin 3 (23% 10 = 3)

			23						

33 should be placed in bin 3 (33% 10 = 3), but it is full.
The step size will be 2 (7 - 33% 7), so try bin 5 next.

			23		33				

43 should be placed in bin 3 (43% 10 = 3), but it is full.
The step size will be 6 (7 - 43% 7), so try bin 9 next.

			23		33				43

53 should be placed in bin 3 (53% 10 = 3), but it is full.
The step size will be 3 (7 - 53% 7), so try bin 6 next.

			23		33	53			43

Since collisions have a different step value, they will not always land in the same order. The complexity of setting up doubling hashing is counterbalanced by its ability to avoid collisions.

Various probing methods can be used depending on the specific details of the situation. Linear probing is fast, but only in cases where the load factor is low. Quadratic probing helps avoid clustering when the load factor is fairly high. Double hashing is best for large datasets in tables with a high load factor.

6.2.2 Hash Functions

Another method of avoiding collisions is to use a good hash function. In general, when hashing values, we need to ensure that the function gives back consistent values so that when we store the value and try to retrieve it, we get the same hash value. Otherwise, we would be looking in the wrong bin.

Our function must distribute the values with a uniform distribution to avoid collisions as much as possible. Clusters in our data will lower the performance as values will not be where we expect them. Our function should be efficient to avoid creating a bottleneck in our program. It also should be scalable, continuing to be efficient as the dataset grows. Finally, the function should not rely on patterns in the data. Overly relying on patterns could lead to issues as the data grows and patterns change.

Here are some methods of hashing:

A) Simple modular hashing

So far, we have looked at simple modular hashing, where we used the modulus to determine the bin value.

```
def simple_modular_hash(key, table_size):
    return key % table_size
```

This method is simple to understand and implement, but can lead to clustering if the input values share common factors.

B) Mid-square hashing

For values which we know are clustered, we can use mid-square hashing: a process by which we square the value and extract the middle digits before using modulo.

```
def __mid_square_hash(key, table_size):
    squared = key **2
    squared_str = str(squared)
    digits = len(squared_str)

    #get the length of digits
    # to extract from the middle
    extract_len = min(len(str(key)), digits)

    #get the middle and starting point
    middle = digits // 2
    start = middle - (extract_len // 2)
    start = min(start, digits - extract_len)

    mid_digits = int(
        squared_str[start:start + extract_len]
        )


    return mid_digits % table_size
```

This technique is useful when input values are clustered around specific values. Another method of avoiding clustering is by using multiplicative hashing. This involves multiplying the value by a decimal value and extracting the fractional part of the result. The fractional part is multiplied by the table size and converted to an integer to find the bin number. In this example, we are using the decimal approximation of the golden ratio, but other constants can also be used.

```
def multi_hash(key, size, constant=0.6180339887):
    hash_value = key * constant
    fractional_part = hash_value - int(hash_value)
    return int(size * fractional_part)
```

Table 6.4 shows how the keys 20, 21, 22, 23, and 24 are distributed in a 10 bin hash table using the methods described above.

Table 6.4 **Hash values of keys 20–24 using different hashing methods**

Key	Modular Hash	Mid-Square Hash	Multiplicative Hash
20	20 % 10 = 0	400 → 0 → 0 % 10 = 0	20 x 0.6180339887 = 12.360679774 int(0.360679774 x 10) = 3
21	21 % 10 = 1	441 → 4 → 4 % 10 = 4	21 x 0.6180339887 = 12.9787137627 int(0.9787137627 x 10) = 9
22	22 % 10 = 2	484 → 8 → 8 % 10 = 8	22 x 0.6180339887 =13.5967477514 int(0.5967477514 x 10) = 5
23	23 % 10 = 3	529 → 2 → 2 % 10 = 2	23 x 0.6180339887 =14.2147817401 int(0.2147817401 x 10) = 2
24	24 % 10 = 4	576 → 7 → 7 % 10 = 7	24 x 0.6180339887 =14.8328157288 int(0.8328157288 x 10) = 8

It is important to understand that real-world data often has patterns built into it, which can lead to poorly distributed hash values. A good hash function can lead to a more distributed hash table. A good distribution is useful for minimizing collisions, optimizing memory usage, maintaining efficiency and scalability, and supporting predictable and high-performance operations.

6.3 Implementing Hash Tables

In Python, dictionaries are a special implementation of hash tables. Simply using a dictionary would abstract away too many details, so we will focus more on building them from the ground up. As discussed previously, there are many ways to implement a hash table, but we will use open-addressing with a simple modular hashing and linear probing. We will build in key-value pairs, as this would be the more common way of using hash tables.

The general setup is as follows:

```
class HashTable:
    def __init__(self, size=10):
        """Initialize the hash table."""
        self.size = size
        self.table = [None] * size
        self.tombstone = '<DELETED>'


    def _hash(self, key):
        """Return hash index using modular hashing."""
        return hash(key) % self.size
```

We are using hash(key) to ensure that all values passed in are converted into a reasonable, well-distributed integer value. If the value is already an integer, hash() will return the integer unchanged.

If we wanted to use a more complex hash function, we could simply replace our hash method here. For example, if we wanted to use mid-square hashing, we could rewrite the hash method as follows. It's a little more complex as we convert the numerical value to a string in order to find the middle.

```python
def _hash(key, table_size):
    """
    Return hash index using
    mid-square hashing.
    """

    squared = key **2
    squared_str = str(squared)
    digits = len(squared_str)

    #get the length of digits
    # to extract from the middle
    extract_len = min(len(str(key)), digits)

    #get the middle and starting point
    middle = digits // 2
    start = middle - (extract_len // 2)
    start = min(start, digits - extract_len)

    mid_digits = int(
        squared_str[start:start + extract_len]
    )

    return mid_digits % table_size
```

For simplicity, we will be using modular hashing unless otherwise stated.

The insertion logic follows what was described in the earlier section. First, we calculate the hash value and use a for loop to probe through the entire table if necessary. If the hash index is empty or a tombstone, we record the value and exit the loop. We also add the condition that if the key is already recorded that we update the value associated with the key. If the table is full, we raise an Exception.

In order to make our HashTable class more robust, we are also allowing no value to be passed in. In the case that the value is not provided, it is assigned to a default value of None and reassigned the value of the key. This allows us to handle both cases like the previous examples and also the more practical examples that follow in the next section.

```
def insert(self, key, value=None):
    """
    Insert a key-value pair into the hash table.
    """
    index = self._hash(key)
    if value is None:
      value = key
    for _ in range(self.size):
      if (
        self.table[index] in (None, self.tombstone)
        or self.table[index][0] == key
      ):
        self.table[index] = (key, value)
        return
      index = (index + 1) % self.size
    raise Exception("Hash table is full")
```

To retrieve values, we again calculate the hash of the key and follow through the loop in the same way as insertion. Unlike Python's built-in dictionary, we can return None if the key is not in the hash map, although this is a choice.

```
def get(self, key):
  """Retrieve value by key."""
  index = self._hash(key)
  for _ in range(self.size):
    if self.table[index] is None:
      return None
    if (
      self.table[index] != self.tombstone
      and self.table[index][0] == key
    ):
      return self.table[index][1]
    index = (index + 1) % self.size
  return None
```

Finally, for deletion, we follow the same logic, returning True or False to indicate if the key-value pair was successfully deleted.

```
def delete(self, key):
  """
  Delete a key-value pair by setting
  a tombstone marker.
  """
  index = self._hash(key)
  for _ in range(self.size):
    if self.table[index] is None:
      return False
```

```
if (
    self.table[index] != self.tombstone
    and self.table[index][0] == key
    ):
    self.table[index] = self.tombstone
    return True
    index = (index + 1) % self.size
return False
```

This implementation will also allow us to explore applications of hash tables.

6.4 Hash Table-Based Algorithms

The main use of hash tables is to quickly look up data. Beyond this simple case, however, there are some common situations where hash tables can be quite useful.

6.4.1 Detecting Duplicates in Data

Oftentimes, we want to detect duplicate values in our data. For example, consider if we had a set of integer values such as:

17	82	9	14	15	38	17	12	35	38

A brute force solution would be to use a nested for loop to cycle through the set of values, comparing each one to see if we have a match. At this point, we should understand that this would have a time complexity of $O(n^2)$ and really should be able to be approached more elegantly.

One such method is using a hash table. In this way, we can add each element to a hash table. If there is a collision with the same value, we know there is a duplicate.

Ideally, with a properly sized table and a good hash table, we shouldn't have many collisions, leading us to a time complexity of O(n), which is much more reasonable. We would, however, have additional space complexity of O(n) since we need to generate the hash table.

To do this, we will assume we already have our HashTable class implemented. The first step is to create a hash table twice the size of our data. This ensures minimal collisions. Then we loop through the data, checking to see if it is in the hash table and adding it if it is not. Should we find a duplicate value, we return True. If we make it through the data without finding a duplicate, we return False.

Rather than writing this as a method of the HashTable class, it can be a standalone function, as long as the class is imported.

```
def duplicateValue(nums):
    ht = HashTable(len(nums)*2)
    for num in nums:
        if ht.get(num):
            return True
        else:
            ht.insert(num)
    return False
```

It is worth noting that in Python, we can quickly determine duplicates by using sets, however, sets are not included in all programming languages and do not help illustrate our knowledge of data structures.

6.4.2 Counting Values

Suppose we want to track how many of a particular value we have. This could be for an inventory system or tallying votes. Often in Python programming, we use dictionaries for this purpose, so it shouldn't be surprising that we can use our custom hash table class as well. The logic will be the same as using a built-in dictionary.

First, we will create an empty hash table to hold our data. It will be set up to store the element as the key and the number of times we've seen it as the value. We will then loop through the data to see if the element is stored as a key in our hash table. If it is, we increment the value. If not, we will add the key with a value of 1.

Knowing a little bit about our data can help us choose a smaller-than-normal hash table since there will likely be duplicates in our data. For example, if we were doing inventory, our hash table size could be based on the number of available inventory items instead of the number of values. For voting, it could be based on the number of candidates instead of the number of votes cast. This keeps our tables small while avoiding collisions. We will write our function to be more generic and base the table size on the total data, since determining the number of unique values would add time complexity.

If we were using an iterable object like a list or a tuple, we could set the size to twice the length and loop through. Since our search and insertion operations take constant time complexity, we can reasonably expect this to have $O(n)$ time complexity due to looping through the iterable and $O(n)$ space complexity due to the construction of the hash table. Returning the entire hash table allows the end user to look up the counts of any item without having to run the function again.

```
def iterable_count(iterable):
  ht = HashTable(size=len(iterable) * 2)
  for item in iterable:
    count = ht.get(item)
  if count is None:
    ht.insert(item, 1)
  else:
    ht.insert(item, count + 1)
  return ht
```

A common application of this is to count the number of occurrences of a word in a body of text. This is the same concept, however, we would have to use the split method to break the text into a list.

```
def word_count(text):
  ht = HashTable(size=len(text.split()) * 2)
  for word in text.split():
    word = word.lower()
    count = ht.get(word)
  if count is None:
    ht.insert(word, 1)
  else:
    ht.insert(word, count + 1)
  return ht
```

6.4.3 Two Sum Problem

A more specific problem is to find a set of numbers in a list that add up to a particular target value. This is used to find complementary values in a variety of settings. For instance, a person may be using a gift card to make a purchase, and we may want to suggest pairs of items they could buy.

The brute force method would be to loop through the list of available values twice. Without any optimization, this would have a worst case $O(n^2)$ time complexity, as we need to check our first value against every other value to see if we match up to the target value. If not, we would need to compare the second value to every other value and continue until we find a match or run out of items. If we could find a way to eliminate the double loop, we would greatly improve the efficiency of this solution.

There are multiple ways to improve this, but using a hash table is an efficient method. The general idea is to go through the loop checking to see if the complementary value is already stored in the table. Since we can efficiently add and look up values in the hash table, we would simply need to go through the loop once, making the time complexity $O(n)$. We do have the additional trade-off of having to create the table, so the space complexity is $O(n)$.

```
def two_sum(nums, target):
  ht = HashTable(size=len(nums) * 2)
  for i, num in enumerate(nums):
    complement = target - num
    index = ht.get(complement)
    if index is not None:
      return [index, i]
    ht.insert(num, i)
  return None
```

6.5 Practical Application - Caching

Caching is a method for storing frequently accessed data in an easy-to-access location. While used in many different areas, a common use case is for storing URLs and a copy of the content on the last view. As we should know by now, there is almost always a trade-off. While caching can speed up the loading of web pages, it also takes up more memory, therefore, we need to be able to limit the number of cached pages. By removing pages that we haven't recently visited, we can keep the memory usage low.

Hash tables can help with this task by allowing us to quickly determine if a web page is in the cache. Since the lookup, insertion, and deletion occur in O(1) time complexity, we have an efficient data structure for this task.

To handle this, we will create a WebCache class. Within the class, we will need to keep track of the cache, which will be an instance of our HashTable class. We will also need to track the order of the pages being added in order to remove the oldest when our hash table reaches a load factor of around 0.7. We can set the capacity as an attribute.

```
class WebCache:
    def __init__(self, size=3):
        self.cache = HashTable(size=size)
        self.order = []
        self.capacity = size
```

Our two main methods would be get_page() and store_page(). To get the page, we try to retrieve it from the cache by passing in the URL. If nothing is returned, then the page is not currently stored and will have to be loaded from the server. In a full web browser implementation, the page content would be loaded and cached back to the hash table. If the content is found, the URL needs to be removed and re-added to our order list. This allows us to keep more recently viewed pages in the cache for faster retrieval. The content is then returned to the browser for faster loading.

Before storing a page, we have to check to see if the URL is already stored and if the cache is at capacity. If the URL is already stored, we remove its current location in the order and add it back to the end to make sure it is stored longer. If the page is not cached, we first check if the cache is at capacity. If it is, we pop the oldest URL, found at index 0, and delete it from the hash table. Once there is room in the cache, we add the content to the cache and add the URL to our order list.

```
def store_page(self, url, content):
    if self.cache.get(url) is not None:
        self.order.remove(url)
    else:
        if len(self.order) >= self.capacity:
            oldest = self.order.pop(0)
            self.cache.delete(oldest)

        self.cache.insert(url, content)
        self.order.append(url)
```

To use this, we create our cache. For this example, we will keep it small to see how.

```
cache = WebCache(size = 2)
cache.store_page(
    "google.com",
    "Google Homepage"
)
```

```
cache.store_page(
  "vibrantpublishers.com",
  "Vibrant Publishers Homepage"
)
print(cache.get_page("google.com"))
#Output: Google Homepage
cache.store_page(
  "github.com",
  "GitHub Homepage"
)
print(cache.get_page("vibrantpublishers.com"))
#Output: Page Not Found
```

While some of the complex details of web browser implementation are overly simplified here, this example should help us see how hash tables can be used to speed up web browsing by storing temporary copies of web content. Like most situations, there is a trade-off, since we gain speed by using more memory to store the content. If we were to use an inefficient algorithm to look up the stored values, we could lose the speed we were trying to gain, making the extra memory use pointless.

Hash tables are an incredibly powerful data structure, offering O(1) time complexity for lookups, insertions, and deletions on average. By using effective collision resolution techniques, we can maintain efficiency, even with large data sets. While not the best tool for every problem their speed and versatility make them an essential part of any programmer's toolkit.

Chapter Summary

- Hash tables provide efficient data storage and retrieval by using hash functions to compute the expected index.

- Collisions occur when multiple keys map to the same bin. Collisions can be handled through chaining (linked lists stored in bins) or open addressing (probing to find the next available bin).

- Various probing techniques, including linear probing, quadratic probing, and double hashing, can be used to handle collisions in open addressing.

- Good hash functions ensure uniform distribution, reducing clustering and minimizing collisions.

Quiz

1. **What is the main advantage of a hash table over arrays and linked lists?**
   a. Hash tables use less memory
   b. Hash tables maintain sorted data
   c. Hash tables have O(1) average-time lookups
   d. Hash tables do not require a hash function

2. **What happens when two keys hash to the same index in a hash table?**
   a. A collision occurs
   b. The table is resized
   c. The second key is ignored
   d. The second key overwrites the first

3. **Which is a collision resolution technique involving linked lists?**
   a. Chaining
   b. Mid-square hashing
   c. Open addressing
   d. Quadratic probing

4. **What is the time complexity of inserting an element into a well-designed hash table?**
   a. O(1)
   b. O(n)
   c. O(log n)
   d. O(n²)

5. **Which probing technique is most prone to clustering?**
    a. Chaining
    b. Double probing
    c. Linear probing
    d. Quadratic probing

6. **Which is not a valid use case for a hash table?**
    a. Counting word frequencies
    b. Detecting duplicates
    c. Implementing caching
    d. Sorting elements

7. **If a hash table has a size of 10, which bin would 25 be placed into, assuming modular hashing?**
    a. 0
    b. 2
    c. 5
    d. 9

8. **Which is a disadvantage of chaining?**
    a. It cannot store key-value pairs.
    b. It does not allow insertions.
    c. It does not handle collisions.
    d. It requires extra memory by storing extra pointers.

9. **What is the purpose of a tombstone?**
    a. To prevent breaking the probing sequence
    b. To reduce memory usage
    c. To speed up insertion
    d. To temporarily store deleted values

10. **What is the advantage of double hashing over quadratic probing?**
    a. Double hashing avoids secondary clustering
    b. Double hashing does not require a prime-sized table
    c. Double hashing does not require rehashing
    d. Double hashing is always faster

Answers

1 – c	2 – a	3 – a	4 – a	5 – c
6 – d	7 – c	8 – d	9 – a	10 – a

CHAPTER 7

Trees

Key Learning Objectives

- Understand tree structures, including root, leaf, and height concepts.
- Explore different types of trees, including binary trees, binary search trees, and tries.
- Understand traversal methods such as Depth-First Search and Breadth-First Search.
- Implement common tree operations like insertion, deletion, and searching.
- Understand practical applications of trees.

In this chapter, we explore trees, a hierarchical data structure used for efficient searching, sorting, and data organization. They are used in various areas, from file systems to artificial intelligence. Understanding their structure and traversal methods enhances our abilities in many computational tasks.

7.1 Introduction to Trees

Trees are a fundamental data structure in computer science. They are used widely for organizing and managing hierarchical data. They are similar to linked lists in that there are nodes connected by edges, however they are non-linear in that they can branch off in different directions. This can allow for more efficient searching, sorting, and hierarchical representation.

The tree data structure is similar to an actual tree in that there is a root node that branches out to other nodes, known as child nodes. A node with no children is known as a leaf.

Figure 7.1 shows a basic tree structure with circles representing nodes and arrows representing edges.

Figure 7.1 **A basic tree structure**

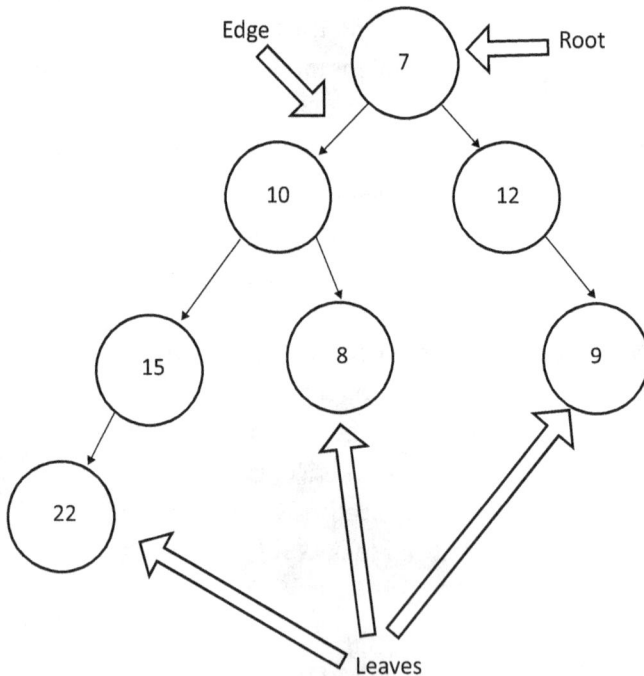

Using Figure 7.1 as an example, we can dive into some of the terminology of trees. The node labeled 7 is the root. It serves as a starting place for the tree. The root can be easily identified as it has no parent node.

The node labeled as 10 has the root as a parent and two children: 15 and 8. All nodes, other than the root, have exactly 1 parent. Nodes with both a parent and at least one child, such as 15 in the diagram, are known as internal nodes.

The tree itself has a height, which is the number of edges from the root to the farthest away node. In this example, 22 is the furthest away, so the height is 3. Another commonly used term is depth. Depth is the number of edges from the root to a specific node. In this diagram, the node labelled 12 has a depth of 1, and 9 has a depth of 2. 22, 8, and 9 are the leaves since they have no children. Having an understanding of the terminology can help demystify the structure and behavior of trees.

There are various types of trees, each of which is suited for different applications. Table 7.1 outlines the differences.

| Table 7.1 | Types of trees |

Tree type	Description
General tree	A tree where each node can have any number of children.
Binary tree	A tree where each node has at most two children.
N-ary tree	A tree where each node can have at most N children.
Balanced tree	A tree where no branch grows significantly deeper than any other.
Unbalanced tree	A tree where some branches grow significantly deeper than others.
Self-Balancing tree	A tree that adjusts its structure to remain balanced.

Given the non-linear structure of trees, we can use them for a variety of tasks. Consider the structure of a web page, for example. There are elements nested within other elements, which may have their own elements nested within them. This type of data could potentially be represented as a list of lists, but it would be difficult to set up and maintain. The tree structure would allow us not only to set it up, but also to add and delete information as necessary. Decision trees can be used in artificial intelligence applications involving classification and regression. As we explore trees, we will see some of the options they open up to us.

7.2 Binary Trees

Binary trees are a common starting point for understanding trees. As previously mentioned, binary trees have at most two children. These are often referred to as the left and right nodes, based on their position in the tree diagram. There are multiple types of binary trees, which are classified based on their structures. Table 7.2 provides an overview of these classifications.

7.2.1 Types of Binary Trees

Binary trees are a great starting place for understanding trees due to the limited number of children. This allows us to focus on the fundamental concepts without getting lost in confusing implementations.

Table 7.2   Types of Binary Trees

Full Binary Tree 	Each node has 0 or 2 children.
Complete Binary Tree 	All levels, except maybe the last, are fully filled. The last level is filled from left to right.
Perfect Binary Tree 	Each node has exactly two children, except the leaves, which are all at the same depth.
Balanced Binary Tree 	The height of each branch is at most one different.

Random Binary Tree	Nodes are added without a strict order, so it may not be balanced or complete.
Skewed Tree	A tree where each node has one child, like a linked link. This is typically unintentional.
Binary Search Tree	A specialized tree where child nodes on the left contain lower values than the parent and child nodes on the right contain higher values.

To code our binary trees, we first need a class for our nodes. This will need to contain data, and the left and right children.

```python
class BinaryNode:
    """A node in a binary tree."""
    def __init__(self, data):
        self.data = data
        self.left = None
        self.right = None
```

The class for binary trees simply needs to be initialized with the tree root.

```python
class BinaryTree:
    """
    A general binary tree with common traversal
    and manipulation methods.
    """
    def __init__(self, root_data=None):
        if root_data is not None:
            self.root = BinaryNode(root_data)
        else:
            self.root = None
```

Since binary trees are non-linear, it can be difficult to populate them with data. This tends not to be done with a method but manually in our programs. This gives us more control in the creation of our trees.

Figure 7.2 **An example of a binary tree**

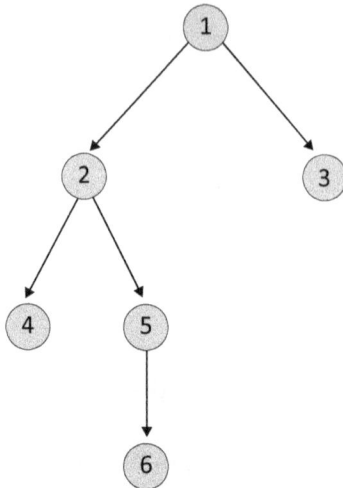

To create the tree seen in Figure 7.2, we would use the following code.

```
bt = BinaryTree(1)
bt.root.left = BinaryNode(2)
bt.root.right = BinaryNode(3)
bt.root.left.left = BinaryNode(4)
bt.root.left.right = BinaryNode(5)
bt.root.left.right.left = BinaryNode(6)
```

This would be unmanageable for large trees, but it will allow us to create small trees without having to worry about any complex details.

7.2.2 Traversing Trees

Since trees, including binary trees, are non-linear, the order in which they are traversed can be subjective. In general, we have depth-first traversal and breadth-first traversal. Since they are primarily used for searching, we call them DFS (depth-first search) and BFS (breadth-first search) even though we also use them for traversal.

A. Depth-first search (DFS)

DFS involves working our way down to the end of a branch and then backtracking to explore other branches. There are three distinct methods of doing this: preorder traversal, inorder traversal, and postorder traversal. The main difference between these is at what point the parent of a subtree is recorded.

Preorder traversal visits the node itself, then its left subtree, and finally its right subtree. Using the tree in Figure 7.2, we start at the root, node 1, and move to the left to node 2 and continue until we reach the end on the left, node 4. At this point our preorder traversal is $1 \rightarrow 2 \rightarrow 4$.

Since we are at the end, we return to the previous node (2) and explore the right, which is node 5. From node 5 we again check the left, which is node 6, and we are at a leaf again. The traversal is now $1 \rightarrow 2 \rightarrow 4 \rightarrow 5 \rightarrow 6$. Note that we did not record "2" since we are simply finishing the left right search from it. We only record the values as we start the search through its subtree.

Node 5's left branch is complete, and it has no right branch, so we move back to node 2. We have already explored its subtree, so back to node 1. Exploring the right branch of node 1. We find 3 and nothing else. The preorder traversal of this tree is $1 \rightarrow 2 \rightarrow 4 \rightarrow 5 \rightarrow 6 \rightarrow 3$.

To implement this in code, we add a method to our BinaryTree class. It starts by printing the node value, then recursively traverses the left subtree, and finally traverses the right subtree.

```
def preorder_traversal(self, node):
    """
    Traverse tree in preorder
    (root-left-right).
    """
    if node:
        print(node.data, end=" → ")
        self.preorder_traversal(node.left)
        self.preorder_traversal(node.right)
```

Assuming we have created our binary tree and have all the necessary classes imported, we can traverse the tree using the root of the tree as the starting point.

```
bt.preorder_traversal(bt.root)
```

Output:

```
1 → 2 → 4 → 5 → 6 → 3 →
```

Inorder and postorder are essentially the same.

For each node, an inorder traversal visits the node's left subtree, the node itself, and then its right subtree, but a postorder traversal visits the node's left subtree, its right subtree, and then the node itself. As you can see, the order in which we record the nodes is different. With an inorder traversal, we wait to record the node until we have fully explored its left branch. Once it is recorded, we then explore its right branch. With a postorder traversal, we wait until we have fully explored both branches, left and right, before we record the node.

```
def inorder_traversal(self, node):
    """
    Traverse tree in inorder
    (left-root-right).
    """
    if node:
        self.inorder_traversal(node.left)
        print(node.data, end=" → ")
        self.inorder_traversal(node.right)
```

Again, following the tree in Figure 7.2, in an inorder traversal, we navigate down the left, not recording any values until we reach the leaf. The first value we record is 4. Then we go back to node 2 and record it before exploring the right path. On the right path, we explore its left and find node 6 as a leaf, and record it as well. We then record node 5 and find nothing on the right. This gives us 4 → 2 → 6 → 5.

We go back up to our root and record its value before exploring the right path. There is only a 3 on the right, so we finish with 4 → 2 → 6 → 5 → 1 → 3.

Postorder traversal records left, right, then root.

```
def postorder_traversal(self, node):
    """
    Traverse tree in postorder
    (left-right-root).
    """
    if node:
        self.postorder_traversal(node.left)
        self.postorder_traversal(node.right)
        print(node.data, end=" → ")
```

However, in a postorder traversal, we work our way down the left, recording 4, but this time we also explore the right branch of node 2 before recording its value, and we do not record 5 until we finish exploring its branches. This gives us $4 \rightarrow 6 \rightarrow 5 \rightarrow 2 \rightarrow 3 \rightarrow 1$.

Each DFS method has its applications. For example, preorder is useful if we want to copy a tree, since it returns the subtree nodes before the branching nodes, allowing us to build the new tree as we traverse it. Postorder is useful for deleting trees since we fully explore to the end of each subtree before accessing the value of a given node. Inorder is commonly used for retrieving values in binary search trees (BSTs).

B. Breadth-first search (BFS)

BFS works its way down the tree level by level, left to right. We frequently use a queue to help with this task. Still using Figure 7.2, we would start by recording the root, node 1, and enqueue nodes 2 and 3, the left and right nodes. Remember that queues work by first in, first out (FIFO), so we dequeue node 2, and record its value. We add its left and right nodes to the queue. At which point, we have 1→2 as our traversal and 3, 4, and 5 in our queue.

We dequeue node 3, record it, and as it has no children, there is nothing to enqueue. The same is true of node 4. Therefore, we now have 1→2→3→4 with only node 5 in the queue.

Removing and recording 5, we enqueue its left node, 6, which we then dequeue and record, noting that it is a leaf.

The final traversal is 1→2→3→4→5→6.

In code form, we create a new queue and loop through until it is empty, adding the left child and right child as we go.

```
def breadth_first_traversal(self):
    """
    Traverse the tree level by level using
    a queue.
    """
    if not self.root:
        return
    queue = Queue()
    queue.enqueue(self.root)
    while not queue.is_empty():
        current = queue.dequeue()
        print(current.data, end=" → ")
        if current.left:
            queue.enqueue(current.left)
        if current.right:
            queue.enqueue(current.right)
```

Unlike DFS, we don't need to pass in the starting node since we always start with the root. As a side note, an iterative version of depth-first search (DFS) is similar in structure to this code, but instead of a queue, we use a stack. This change in data structure causes the nodes to be visited in depth-first order rather than level-by-level.

```
bt.breadth_first_traversal()

Output:
1 → 2 → 3 → 4 → 5 → 6 →
```

There are many applications of BFS, often involving finding the shortest path to some information. We will explore some of these later.

7.2.3 Operations with Binary Trees

Like most data structures, we would like to be able to search, insert, and delete information into our binary trees. While some specialized trees may require different implementations, we will consider that the end goal is to maintain trees that are complete.

To search, we can use any of our traversal methods. There can be some cases where the depth of a tree can cause problems with recursion limits, so we will implement a BFS search or an iterative DFS. This is simpler since there is no recursion and can be easily implemented with a queue.

This method is almost identical to our BFS for traversal; however, we stop early if we find the value we are searching for.

```python
def search(self, data):
    """
    Search for a value in the binary tree
    using BFS."""
    if not self.root:
        return False
    queue = Queue()
    queue.enqueue(self.root)
    while not queue.is_empty():
        current = queue.dequeue()
        if current.data == data:
            return True
        if current.left:
            queue.enqueue(current.left)
        if current.right:
            queue.enqueue(current.right)
    return False
```

The time complexity for using BFS will never be worse than O(n), which would be when the element is the last in the tree, or not in the tree at all. There is some added memory use due to building the queue; however, the space complexity will never go beyond O(n).

Inserting values is also typically done using BFS. Unless there is a specific reason to do otherwise, we insert data at the first unfilled node. If we have a balanced tree, this will be near the end, making the time complexity O(n), but in an unbalanced tree,it would be O(log n) on average.

This insert method would be similar to search, but it would add a node rather than return a value.

```python
def insert(self, data):
    """
    Insert a node into the binary tree at the
    first available position."""
    new_node = BinaryNode(data)
    if not self.root:
        self.root = new_node
        return
    queue = Queue()
    queue.enqueue(self.root)
    while not queue.is_empty():
        current = queue.dequeue()
        if not current.left:
            current.left = new_node
            return
        else:
            queue.enqueue(current.left)
```

```
if not current.right:
  current.right = new_node
  return
else:
  queue.enqueue(current.right)
```

Deletion is a tricky process. Much like with linked lists, we need to update the pointers to the next node. Unfortunately, we may now have multiple child nodes to reassign. The simplest way to handle this potentially cumbersome situation is to replace the node with the last node in BFS. To do this, we will replace the data of the node to be deleted with the value of the last node, rather than worry about having to reconnect parent and child nodes in the correct sequence. We will, however, need to remove all references to the replacement node, including its parent's pointer to it.

This assumes that the relationships between nodes are not important, so its applications are limited. For example, if the tree represents some kind of file structure, it wouldn't make sense to replace a deleted folder with another deeper folder. In this case, we would need some other method, such as removing the entire subtree.

To do this efficiently, we will need to maintain pointers to the node with the value we want to delete, as well as a pointer to the last node, and also one to its parent.

```
def delete(self, data):
    """
    Delete a node from the binary tree by
    replacing it with the last processed
    node in BFS.
    """
```

```
if not self.root:
  return
queue = Queue()
queue.enqueue(self.root)
node_to_delete = None
last_node = None
parent_of_last = None
while not queue.is_empty():
  current = queue.dequeue()
  if current.data == data:
    node_to_delete = current
  if current.left:
    queue.enqueue(current.left)
    parent_of_last = current
    last_node = current.left
  if current.right:
    queue.enqueue(current.right)
    parent_of_last = current
    last_node = current.right
if node_to_delete and last_node:
  node_to_delete.data = last_node.data
  if parent_of_last:
    if parent_of_last.right == last_node:
      parent_of_last.right = None
    else:
      parent_of_last.left = None
```

While a bit of an annoyance, failure to update the parent to the final node would keep it in memory even if the data was to be replaced with null.

The time complexity of deletion, in this manner, is O(n) since we need to run through the entire tree. The space complexity is O(n) as we need to generate the queue.

7.3 Binary Search Trees (BSTs)

A binary search tree is a special type of binary tree. Nodes are arranged such that we can efficiently search for, insert, and delete values. Values in BSTs are arranged so that values on the left are less than the parent node's value, while values on the right are greater. In a standard BST, there should be no repeated values. Figure 7.3 shows a sample binary search tree.

Figure 7.3 **A sample binary tree**

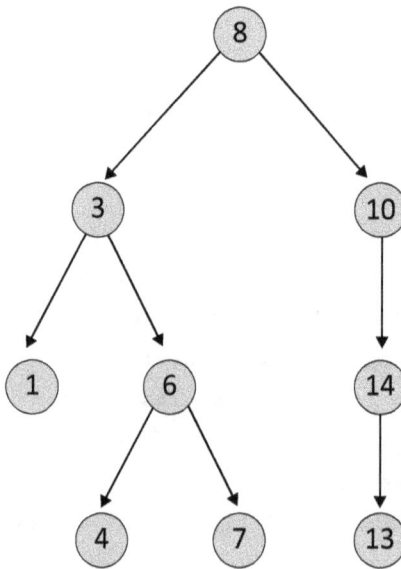

The basic setup of a BST is the same as any binary tree, but we will call the class BinarySearchTree for clarity.

```
class BinaryNode:
    """Represents a node in the Binary Search Tree."""
    def __init__(self, data):
        self.data = data
```

```
      self.left = None
      self.right = None


class BinarySearchTree:
   """Binary Search Tree (BST) implementation."""
   def __init__(self):
      self.root = None
```

7.3.1 Traversal

An interesting feature of a binary search tree is that an inorder traversal will give us the sequence of values in order. Remember that in order traversal goes left-root-right. So even though the tree in Figure 7.3 might seem somewhat oddly sequenced, we can quickly turn it back into the ordered sequence 1, 3, 4, 6, 7, 8, 10, 13, 14 by traversing it. We can also use the other traversal methods; however, they have limited applications for BST and so we will not implement them.

The method for `inorder_traversal` is as follows.

```
def inorder_traversal(self, node=None):
   """
   Perform an inorder traversal and
   print the tree structure.
   """

   if node is None:
     node = self.root
   if node:
     self.inorder_traversal(node.left)
     print(node.data, end=" → ")
     self.inorder_traversal(node.right)
```

Most operations on BSTs are recursive by nature. To abstract away some of the details, we will include an optional node argument. If set to None it will be overwritten by the root. This allows us to write nicer code in the main body of our programs.

7.3.2 Searching

If we wanted to see if the value 14 was in the BST, we would recursively search through the nodes, moving to the left or right if the value is less than or greater than the root. For 14, we look at the root, which is 8. If 14 is in the tree, it would be on the right side. The value on the right is 10, so we look on the right again. Since this value is 14, we know it's in the tree.

We can determine that 5 is not in the tree by the same logic. Checking the root, 8, we know 5 should be on the left. The left is 3, so we check the right, which is 6. The value on the left of 6 is 4. Since node 4 has no left child, 5 is not in the tree.

```
def search(self, data, node=None):
    """Search for a value in the BST."""
    if node is None:
        if self.root is None:
            return None
        node = self.root
    if node is None or node.data == data:
        return node
    if data < node.data and node.left is not None:
        return self.search(data, node.left)
    elif data > node.data and node.right is not None:
        return self.search(data, node.right)
    return None
```

As long as the tree is balanced, each recursive step halves the space for the node to be in, much like binary search for arrays. This gives us an average time complexity of O(log n), or better than linear complexity. If the tree is skewed, we have a worst case of O(n) since we end up visiting all the nodes. The space complexity depends on the recursion depth, which is linked to the height of the tree. On average, this will be O(log h), where h is the height of the tree.

7.3.3 Inserting

Inserting is a similar process, except that we need to find where the value should be. To insert 12 into the tree, we search through moving from 8 to 10 to 14 to 13. We know 12 should be on the left, and since node 13 does not have a left child, we can create a new node and assign it as the left child of 13.

```python
def insert(self, data, node=None):
    """Insert a new node into the BST."""
    if self.root is None:
        self.root = BinaryNode(data)
        return
    if node is None:
        node = self.root
    if data < node.data:
        if node.left is None:
            node.left = BinaryNode(data)
        else:
            self.insert(data, node.left)
    elif data > node.data:
        if node.right is None:
            node.right = BinaryNode(data)
        else:
            self.insert(data, node.right)
```

The complexities mirror those of search for the same reasons as search.

7.3.4 Deletion

Deletion is a real pain in binary search trees. Since the structure of the data in the BST is important, we cannot simply move the last data point to the deleted element's position, however, we can take advantage of the organization to make deletion easier. There are three possible deletion situations, each with its own solution.

A. Node with no children (leaf)

If the node to be deleted has no children, we delete it by removing its parent's reference to it. Python garbage collection removes information without any reference. Figure 7.4 shows this case, deleting the 5.

Figure 7.4 Deleting a leaf (5)

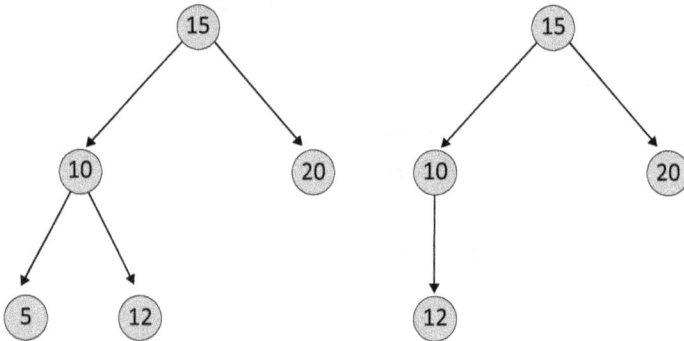

B. Node with one child

If a node has only one child, we can replace the node with the child. This will maintain the structure of the overall BST since the subtrees are also binary search trees. Figure 7.5 shows this case, deleting the 20.

Figure 7.5 Deleting a node with one child (20)

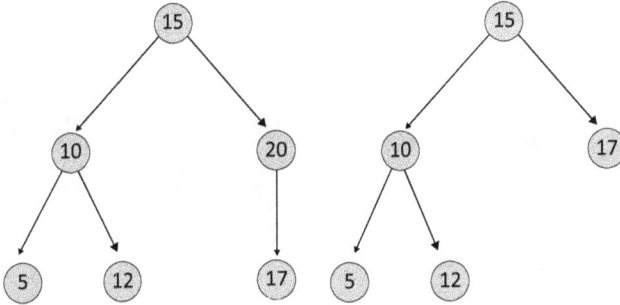

C. Node with two children

For a node with two children, we replace the node with the next largest value in the tree. Due to the structure of a BST, it will always be the smallest value in the right subtree of the node we are deleting. If this node has children, we also need to update their references. Figure 7.6 shows this case, deleting the 10.

Figure 7.6 Deleting a node with two children (10)

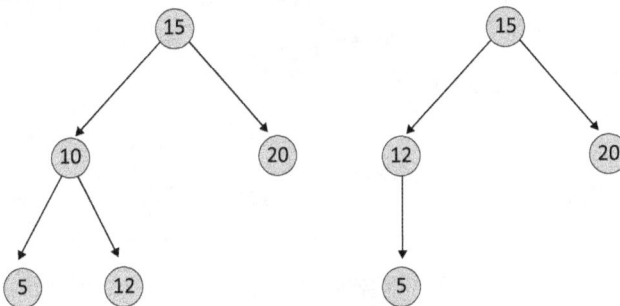

Our delete method will need to handle each of these cases separately, returning the replacement node or None if one does not exist.

```
def delete(self, data, node=None):
  """Delete a node from the BST."""
  if node is None:
    node = self.root
  if node is None:
    return None
  if data < node.data:
    node.left = self.delete(data, node.left)
  elif data > node.data:
    node.right = self.delete(data, node.right)
  else:
    if node.left is None and node.right is None:
      return None
    elif node.left is None:
      return node.right
    elif node.right is None:
      return node.left
    else:
      successor = self._min_value_node(node.right)
      node.data = successor.data
      node.right = self.delete(
        successor.data,
        node.right
      )
  return node
```

Case 3 is where things get interesting. We need a method to find the minimum value to replace the deleted node. This method continues down the left branches until we find the final left value. Due to the structure of the BST, the final leftmost node will be the lowest value.

```
def _min_value_node(self, node):
    """
    Find the node with the smallest value
    in a subtree.
    """
    current = node
    while current.left is not None:
        current = current.left
    return current
```

We recursively delete any node that we use to replace the deleted node.

Again, our time and space complexities are the same. Having complexities in the O(log n) range makes binary search trees more efficient than general binary trees; however, they cannot be used for all applications.

7.4 Tree-Based Algorithms

7.4.1 Expression trees

An expression tree is a binary tree where we store mathematical expressions. This could be something as simple as 1 + 2, as seen in Figure 7.7, or something more complex such as (3 +5) x 2 - 8, as seen in Figure 7.8.

Figure 7.7 1 + 2 represented as an expression tree

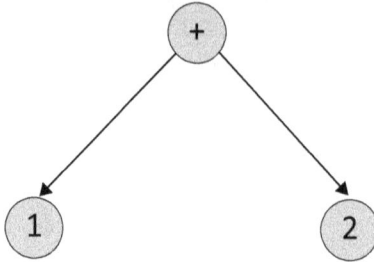

Figure 7.8 (3 +5) x 2 - 8 represented as an expression tree

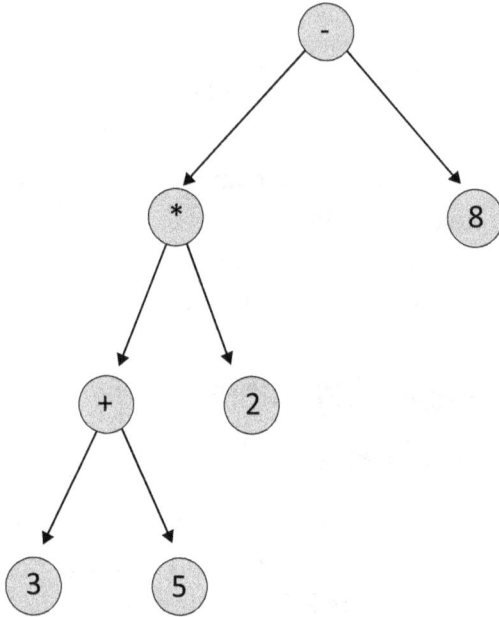

We'll try to keep the mathematics simple here, but an understanding of order of operations is necessary to understand the structure of the trees being created. We structure the tree in such a way that the operators at the top are the last to be completed and those at the bottom are first. Table 7.3 shows the order of operations, often shortened to PEMDAS, or as you may remember from grade school, "Please excuse my dear Aunt Sally."

Table 7.3	Order of operations

Parthethesis
Exponents
Multiplication and Division
Addition and Subtraction

In an expression tree, we have expressions and operators. A special kind of expression is a literal number (e.g. 10, 5, etc.) Literal numbers are always leaves in the tree. Operators always have one or two children, their operands, each of which is an expression tree. We need an algorithm for evaluating the expressions in these trees. The basic idea would be to get the values of the operands, and then apply the operand. This left-right-root sequence matches postorder traversal.

While we could write a new class for expression trees, we'll just reuse our BinaryTree class and add in an evaluate method.

```
def evaluate(self, node=None):
    """
    Evaluate an arithmetic expression tree using
    postorder traversal.
    """
    if node is None:
        node = self.root
```

```
if node.left is None and node.right is None:
    return int(node.data)
left_value = self.evaluate(node.left)
right_value = self.evaluate(node.right)
if node.data == '+':
    return left_value + right_value
elif node.data == '-':
    return left_value - right_value
elif node.data == '*':
    return left_value * right_value
elif node.data == '/':
    return left_value / right_value
return 0
```

As with our previous postorder traversal, we use recursion to go through the tree. If we find a leaf, we know it is a numerical value to be returned, however, any other node will require some arithmetic operation.

This is a fairly elegant algorithm since it takes advantage of the tree's structure and the way recursive calls return values from the bottom up. It also has good time complexity, O(n), due to the evaluation of each node, and decent space complexity, O(n), based on the size of the recursion stack.

7.4.2 Tries (Prefix trees)

Prefix trees are a non-binary tree structure that can be used for spell checking and auto-complete. Non-binary trees have the same central logic as binary trees, however, we cannot discuss them in terms of left and right children. Instead, each node will have an array of children without any specific direction. This is useful for more complex structures such as tries. Since our focus in this chapter is on binary trees, we need to look at a simple implementation of a non-binary tree. For our prefix tree, we will only worry about using an insert method to build the tree and a search word to see if the word is contained in the tree.

For simplicity, we will use a dictionary for storing the child nodes in our TrieNode class, although we could use our custom HashTable class. This is to allow us to quickly look up the children, which is important as we could have children for up to each letter of the alphabet. We also store an attribute to determine if we are at the end of a word. This is necessary in case we have words which contain other words, such as Java and JavaScript.

Our Trie class will store an empty node at a starting point, which will act as an entry point to all of the subtrees.

```
class TrieNode:
    """A node in the Trie data structure."""
    def __init__(self):
        self.children = {}
        self.is_end_of_word = False


class Trie:
    """Trie (prefix tree) implementation."""
    def __init__(self):
        self.root = TrieNode()
```

Figure 7.9 shows a sample trie containing the words car, cap, cat, and cake.

Figure 7.9 A sample trie

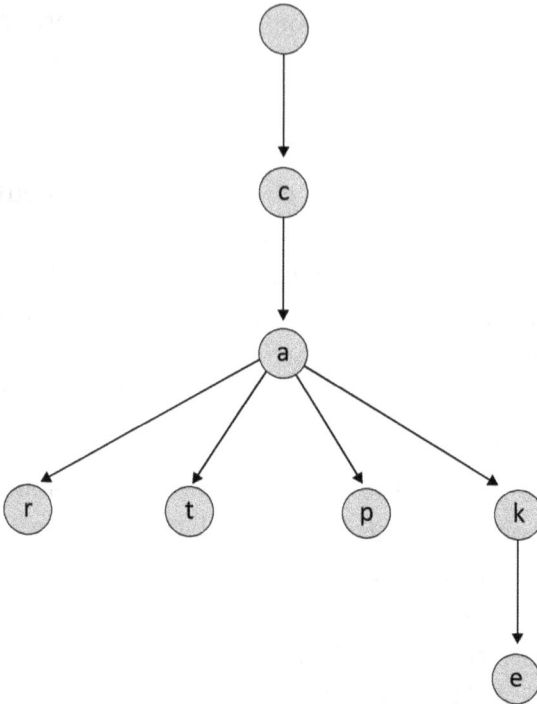

To build the tree, we need an insert method. This method works through the words letter by letter and builds out the trie, checking to see if the next letter is already the child of the previous letter. If not, we add it and move on. Once we hit the end of a work, we mark it as an end. This allows us to store words with the same prefixes in the same branch. For example, we would store the words car, carp, and carpet in the same branch, just marking the 'r', 'p', and 't' as ending points of the word.

```
def insert(self, word):
    """Insert a word into the trie."""
    node = self.root
    for char in word:
        if char not in node.children:
            node.children[char] = TrieNode()
        node = node.children[char]
    node.is_end_of_word = True
```

If we were building a spell checker or a dictionary for a word game, we would need to be able to find out if our word is stored in the trie. To do this we would navigate down through the trie, checking the children of each node to see if the next letter is stored there. The final step is the clever bit. If all the letters are connected in sequence, we next make sure that it is recorded as the end of a word. This ensures that the word is a whole match and not a match with a prefix. For example, if we stored "python" in a trie and searched "pyth" all the letters would match, but "h" would not be the end of the word, so "pyth" is not included.

```
def search(self, word):
    """Check if a word exists in the Trie."""
    node = self.root
    for char in word:
        if char not in node.children:
            return False
        node = node.children[char]
    return node.is_end_of_word
```

Another trie application is an autocomplete feature. While modern autocomplete programs would likely have more complicated logic, the basic idea is to predict the next letters that would complete the word. First, we would need a method to determine if what we have typed so far is in the trie. Much like the search method, we loop through the characters in the prefix and ensure that the nodes are all connected in the branch. We are no longer concerned with the end of the word, so we ignore that. Finally, if the prefix is in the tree, we return the last node of the prefix. This will give us the subtree of all of the available words that could be made from the given prefix.

```python
def starts_with(self, prefix):
    """
    Return the node at the end of the
    prefix if it exists.
    """
    node = self.root
    for char in prefix:
        if char not in node.children:
            return None
        node = node.children[char]
    return node
```

We'll also need a method to compile the list of possible words, which we'll call autocomplete. This method will call starts_with to get the ending node, and then use DFS to travel down each branch to find all of the available words before returning them as a list. When we looked at binary trees we used recursion to handle DFS, however since some words can be quite lengthy, the height of the trie, and therefore the depth of the recursion, can be memory intensive. While we could technically use recursion to reach the end of "pneumonoultramicroscopicsilicovolcanoconiosis", the performance of a large dictionary of long words would suffer.

To overcome this issue, we can reuse our Stack class which we used for DFS in maze navigation. Whenever we find a node marked as the end of a word, we record it as a word.

```python
def autocomplete(self, prefix):
    """
    Return a list of words that start
    with the given prefix.
    """
    start_node = self.starts_with(prefix)
    if not start_node:
        return []
    results = []
    stack = Stack()
    stack.push((start_node, prefix))
    while not stack.is_empty():
        node, word = stack.pop()
        if node.is_end_of_word:
            results.append(word)
        for char, child_node in node.children.items():
            stack.push((child_node, word + char))
    return results

#sample usage
trie = Trie()
words = [
    "apple","app","apply","banana",
    "band","bandwidth","bat","batman"
    ]
```

```
for word in words:
    trie.insert(word)

print(trie.autocomplete("app"))
#Output: ['app','apply','apple']

print(trie.autocomplete("ban"))
#Output: ['band','bandwidth','banana']

print(trie.autocomplete("bat"))
#Output: ['bat','batman']

print(trie.autocomplete("xyz"))
#Output: []
```

The time complexity of this autocomplete method depends on both the prefix and the number of words that need to be returned. Luckily, finding the prefix is linear and can be referred to as O(m) complexity, where m is the length of the prefix. Since we have to traverse the subtree, which also happens in linear time. This time, it depends on how many branches there are, so we can refer to it as O(k). Combining these gives us O(m+k) time complexity. It may be tempting to write this as O(n), however, this glosses over the details of the algorithm.

The space complexity depends on the size of the stack being generated during the autocomplete method. Since the stack grows based on the number of works returned, we can call this O(k), where k is the number of words.

This is considerably more efficient than brute force looping through a list of words to find matches to the prefix. In that case you would need to not only loop through the whole list, but also through each word which would definitely take much longer as it would be based on the entire list, not just the parts that share the prefix.

7.5 Practical Application - File Systems

Folders and files are typically stored in a tree structure for more efficient storage and retrieval. While we are unlikely to code our own operating system, working through the logic can provide us with valuable insight into how trees can be a useful structure.

First, let's consider the structure of a file system. We have a root directory which can contain files and folders. The folders can contain their own files and other folders. Right away we can see leaves and inner nodes: the files and folders. However, an empty folder would still be considered a leaf node. We should also understand that a binary tree would not be sensible for this task as each folder can contain more than two files or folders, so this will be more like our trie example in that the children will be stored in a Python dictionary.

```python
class FileNode:
    def __init__(self, name, is_directory=False):
        self.name = name
        self.is_directory = is_directory
        # Dictionary to store subdirectories and files
        self.children = {}
```

The file system itself will need to be initialized with a root attribute set as a directory.

```
class FileSystem:
    def __init__(self):
        self.root = FileNode("root", is_directory=True)
```

We will need several operations that are common in file systems. We need to be able to search for files, insert new files or directories, and delete files or directories. In order to help with the examples, we will use the sample file structure seen in Figure 7.10.

Figure 7.10 **A sample file structure**

```
(root)
├─ home
│  ├─ user
│  │  ├─ docs
│  │  │  ├─ file.txt
│  │  │  ├─ notes.doc
│  │  ├─ music
│  │  │  ├─ song.mp3
```

7.5.1 Searching

Searching through a file system to see if a file exists can be done recursively in a depth first search. We start with the first child of the root and search down through, ignoring any files that are not the target file.

```
def search(self, filename, node=None):
    """
    Searches for a file in the file system using
    DFS.
    """
    if node is None:
        node = self.root
    if filename in node.children:
        return f"Found: {filename}"
    for child in node.children.values():
        if child.is_directory:
            result = self.search(filename, child)
            if result:
                return result
    return "File Not Found"
```

The time complexity of finding a file can be O(n) if the file does not exist and we have to explore all of the nodes, however, it would likely be found earlier. In terms of space complexity, it depends on the recursion depth and it depends on the deepest level of the file structure, represented by d. This makes the space complexity O(d).

7.5.2 Inserting

Our insert method will take the file path to the new file or directory. We will use the same method for both inserting a new file or directory by using an optional argument to determine which we are working with.

```
def insert(self, path, is_directory=False):
    """
    Inserts a file or directory into the
    file system.
    """
    parts = path.strip("/").split("/")
    node = self.root
    for part in parts[:-1]:
        if (part not in node.children or
            not node.children[part].is_directory
        ):
            return "Invalid Path"
        node = node.children[part]
    node.children[parts[-1]] = FileNode(
        parts[-1], is_directory
        )
```

We use the string method split to separate the path into sections, and use the strip method to remove the backspaces. Passing in "home/user/docs/report.pdf" will be separated into ["home", "user", "docs", "report.pdf"]. We need to ensure that all parts of the path are already in the tree, excluding the final part, the file, or the new directory. This is why we loop over parts[:-1]. If the sequence is not in the child nodes, we have an invalid path.

Assuming the path is valid, we add the new file or directory as a child to the final node, setting it as either a file or a dictionary in the process.

In terms of complexity, the time is related to the length of the file path. The worst case would be that the file path is completely valid and we have to navigate to the end of the branch, which would be the typical case. This gives us a time complexity of O(d), where d is the depth of the file path. There is no additional memory used, so the space complexity is O(1).

7.5.3 Deleting

Deletion in a non-binary tree tends to be challenging, however since we are creating a tree that mimics a file structure, we will delete any child nodes attached to any node we are deleting. This removes the need to reassign nodes, which is where the difficulty comes in. We could also return an error if we try to delete a folder that is not empty, however we will code that option.

Again, we can use the same method for both files and directories.

Our logic will be to break down our path into parts, similar to inserting, and ensure the target exists. Once we have successfully navigated to the target, we delete the node. Once the node is deleted, the child will also be deleted since there is no reference to them left in the program, and they will be garbage collected. This makes our method simple to code and very efficient.

```
def delete(self, path):
    """
    Deletes a file or directory and
    all its contents.
    """
    parts = path.strip("/").split("/")
    node = self.root
```

```
# Traverse to the parent directory
for part in parts[:-1]:
  if (
    part not in node.children or
    not node.children[part].is_directory
  ):
    return "Invalid path: No such parent dir"
  node = node.children[part]

# Check if the target exists
if parts[-1] not in node.children:
  return "Error: Path does not exist"

# Delete the file/directory
# and all its contents
del node.children[parts[-1]]
return f"Deleted: {path}"
```

Based on its similarity to the other file structure methods, it should not be surprising that the time complexity is O(d) based on the recursion depth, and the space complexity is O(1) since no new structures are created.

While not a comprehensive file system, this application should help show yet another of the many versatile ways that trees can be used. Their complexity does not make them suitable for all cases; however, for non-linear linked data, they are efficient in both time and space.

Trees have countless applications in computer science and are an essential tool in any programmer's toolkit. These are great in situations where we have a clear starting point for our hierarchical data. Next, we will look at graphs, a similar non-linear structure, which removes this need for a root node.

Chapter Summary

- Trees are hierarchical data structures with nodes connected by edges. Roots have no parent, whereas leaves have no children.

- Binary trees have at most two children per node. Binary Search Trees (BSTs) are a special, sorted type of binary tree.

- Trees are non-linear, so linear search methods are impossible. Depth-First Search (DFS) explores branches fully before backtracking. Breadth-First Search (BFS) processes nodes level by level.

- Tries, also known as prefix trees, enable fast word searches, making them useful for autocomplete and dictionaries.

- Trees have a wide variety of applications, including file systems, search engines, and expression evaluation.

Quiz

1. **What is the root node in a tree?**

   a. The node with no children

   b. The node with no parent

   c. The node with the highest value

   d. The node with two children

2. **What is the height of this tree?**

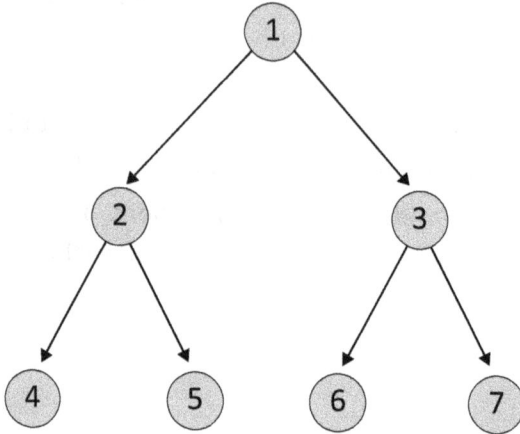

   a. 1

   b. 2

   c. 3

   d. 7

3. **What is a leaf node?**

   a. A node that has at least one child

   b. A node that has exactly two children

   c. A node that has no children

   d. The first node in a tree

4. **What is the main advantage of using a Binary Search Tree?**
   a. Consistently faster insertion and deletion
   b. It always as a balanced structure
   c. It takes up less space than arrays
   d. The ability to store data in sorted order

5. **Which application would be best implemented with a Binary Search Tree?**
   a. Efficiently maintaining a sorted dataset with frequent insertions and deletions
   b. Finding the shortest path in a maze
   c. Implementing an autocomplete system
   d. Organizing and searching hierarchical data like folder structures

6. **Which traversal method visits the left subtree, followed by the root, and then the right subtree?**
   a. Breadth-first
   b. Inorder
   c. Preorder
   d. Postorder

7. **What is the best case time complexity for searching in a Binary Search Tree (BST)?**
   a. O(1)
   b. O(n)
   c. O(log n)
   d. O(n log n)

8. What is the main advantage of using tries (prefix trees)?

   a. Automatic balancing
   b. Avoiding duplicate data
   c. Faster searching
   d. Reduced memory usage

9. Which real-world application is best suited for a tree data structure?

   a. Implementing a stack
   b. Managing a hierarchical file system
   c. Sorting a small list of numbers
   d. Storing linear data in order

10. Which application would be best suited for using a prefix tree?

    a. Implementing a priority queue
    b. Managing hierarchical file systems
    c. Sorting an array of numbers
    d. Storing and searching words efficiently in a dictionary

Answers

1 – b	2 – b	3 – c	4 – d	5 – a
6 – b	7 – c	8 – c	9 – b	10 – d

CHAPTER 8

Graphs

Key Learning Objectives

- Understand graph structures including nodes, edges and weights.
- Explore different types of graphs.
- Understand the different methods of implementing graphs.
- Perform graph traversals.
- Find shortest paths using a variety of algorithms.

In this chapter we explore graphs, a data structure perfect for representing relationships and connections between elements. Graphs can be used to represent social networks, city maps, and dependency resolution in software. Unlike trees, graphs can represent non-hierarchical structures.

8.1 Introduction to Graphs

In the last chapter we looked at trees, a powerful non-linear structure with many applications. Graphs share many characteristics with trees and, in fact, trees can be considered a specialized type of graph. Unlike trees, graphs do not necessarily follow a specific hierarchy and can have a much more complex relationship between elements.

Connections in a social network could be represented as a graph structure. There is no specific starting point, as no one member is more important than any other. Members can be connected to any number of other members, and the connection may not go both ways. Figure 8.1 shows a representation of a simple social network.

Figure 8.1 **A sample graph representing a social network**

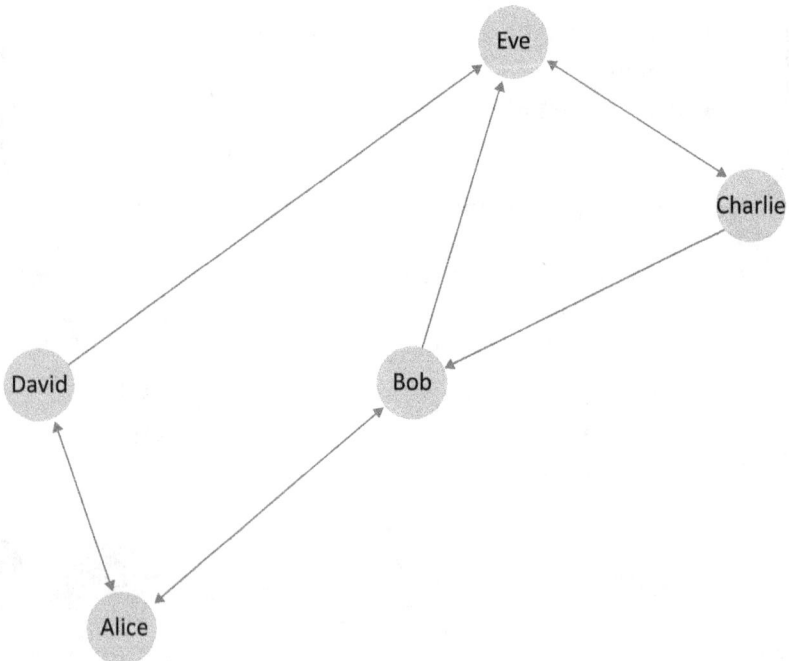

In this graph, the members are nodes, or vertices as they are commonly called. The connections between them are called edges. In a directed graph, such as this one, the arrows show the direction of the relationship. In this specific case, Alice and Bob both follow each other as shown by the double arrow. The arrow on the edge between Bob and Eve shows there is a one way relationship where Bob follows Eve.

In some graphs, edges have weight. There's no weight in the social media graph as there is no value to compare in the connections. In Figure 8.2, the weights represent the distances between cities. These weights can be useful in determining the optimal path between nodes.

Figure 8.2 **An undirected weighted graph representing distances between cities**

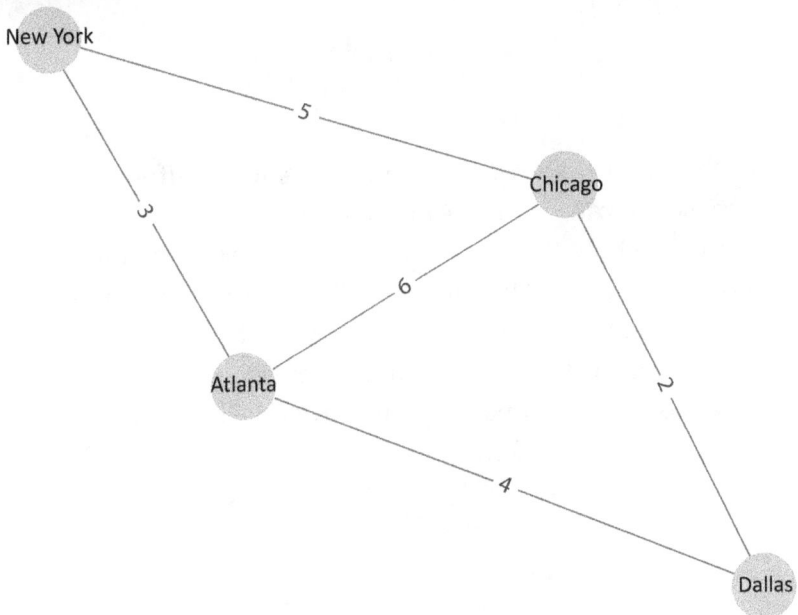

Keeping track of all of the information in a graph can be quite daunting but luckily we have some tools that we can use to keep track.

An adjacency matrix is used to keep track of connections and weights. It is a two dimensional array, which, in Python, can be implemented as either a list of lists or as a NumPy array. In unweighted graphs a 1 indicates a connection while a 0 indicates no connection.

Our adjacency matrix for Alice, Bob, Charlie, David, and Eve would look like this:

adj_matrix_people = [

[0, 1, 0, 1, 0],

[1, 0, 0, 0, 1],

[0, 1, 0, 0, 1],

[1, 0, 0, 0, 1],

[0, 0, 1, 0, 0]

]

Each inner list shows the connections for a different person, so we can see that Alice, the first inner list , is only connected to Bob, the second person and David the fourth. Bob is connected to Alice and Eve, the 1st and 5th people. This ordering is arbitrary as there is no first or second node, other than the order that we enter them into the graph. Note the zeros on the diagonal as people are not connected to themselves. Figure 8.3 shows this as a table.

Figure 8.3 Social network adjacency matrix written as a table

	Alice	Bob	Charlie	David	Eve
Alice	0	1	0	1	0
Bob	1	0	0	0	1
Charlie	0	1	0	0	1
David	1	0	0	0	1
Eve	0	0	1	0	0

In a weighted graph, the value represents the weight of the connection. A zero typically still represents no connection, but some algorithms require including a high value, or infinity, if we are looking for the least costly path.

With the order New York, Chicago, Atlanta, Dallas, our city adjacency matrix would be:

adj_matrix_cities = [

    [0, 5, 3, 0],

    [5, 0, 6, 2],

    [3, 6, 0, 4],

    [0, 2, 4, 0]

]

In our adjacency matrices, we are storing a lot of information about connections that do not exist. In a graph with lots of unconnected vertices, this would lead to a lot of wasted memory. An adjacency list only tracks the connections from each vertex, therefore removing the need of tracking zeroes.

For an unweighted graph, such as our social network we store the connected vertices as a list for each vertex.

```
adj_list_people = [
    [1,3],
    [0,4],
    [1,4],
    [0,4],
    [2]
]
```

We can also store our city connections as a list of lists as before using the same indices. We need to store both the connected vertex and the weight of the edge.

```
adj_list_cities = [
    [(1, 5), (2, 3)],
    [(0, 5), (2, 6), (3, 2)],
    [(0, 3), (1, 6), (3, 4)],
    [(1, 2), (2, 4)]
]
```

Another option, which is more intuitive but less efficient is using a dictionary of dictionaries. This does eliminate the need of tracking which city is assigned to which index, however the large amount of strings stored will use slightly more memory.

```
adj_list_cities = {
    "New York": [("Chicago", 5), ("Atlanta", 3)],
    "Chicago": [("New York", 5), ("Atlanta", 6), ("Dallas", 2)],
    "Atlanta": [("New York", 3), ("Chicago", 6), ("Dallas", 4)],
    "Dallas": [("Chicago", 2), ("Atlanta", 4)]
}
```

Yet another option is an edge list. These are similar to an adjacency list, but instead of having a list for each node we store edges based on the connected nodes.

edge_list_people = [

   (0, 1),

   (0, 3),

   (1, 0),

   (1, 4),

   (2, 1),

   (2, 4),

   (3, 0),

   (3, 4),

   (4, 2)

]

For a weighted graph, we also include the weights.

edge_list_cities = [

   (0, 1, 5),

   (0, 2, 3),

   (1, 2, 6),

   (1, 3, 2),

   (2, 3, 4)

]

Again, for clarity we can include the names as strings for readability, however this is less efficient.

```
edge_list_cities = [
    ("New York", "Chicago", 5),
    ("New York", "Atlanta", 3),
    ("Chicago", "Atlanta", 6),
    ("Chicago", "Dallas", 2),
    ("Atlanta", "Dallas", 4)
]
```

Since we have three different ways to store the information, we need to know which one to choose for our situation. In some cases, the choice is not ours to make. Some of the algorithms which we will discuss later are built around a particular stored method, often edge list. If this is the case, we choose whichever the algorithm is built around.

In any other case, we need to consider the nature of the graph. We need to see how many vertices and edges we have and consider how dense the connections are. For an adjacency matrix, we store a value for each vertex compared to every other vertex, giving $O(V^2)$ space complexity, where V is the number of vertices. If we have a sparsely connected graph we would be storing information for vertices which are not connected. Figure 8.4 shows a dense graph where each vertex has multiple edges.

Figure 8.4　A dense graph appropriate for an adjacency matrix

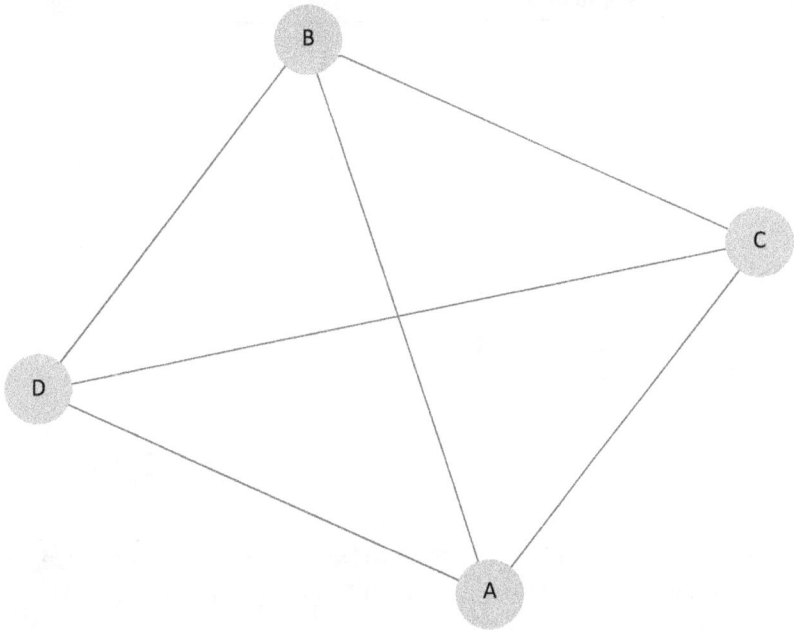

For an adjacency list we are storing a list for each vertex and their edges, so we have to consider the space the vertices and edges take up, giving us $O(V + E)$. For sparsely connected graphs, this would be more efficient, but not if the number of edges grows more dense. Figure 8.5 shows a graph with limited edges compared to the number of vertices.

Figure 8.5 A minimally connected graph appropriate for an adjacency list

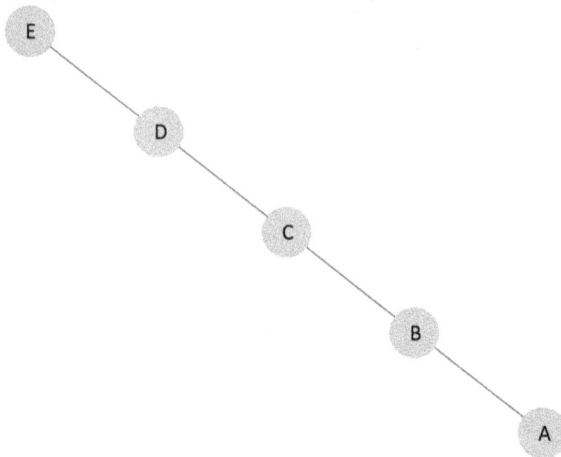

An edge list has the potential to be very efficient as we are only storing edges. This gives us O(E) space complexity as long as the number of edges is not greater than V². Figure 8.6 shows a spare graph with a limited number of vertices and edges.

Figure 8.6 A sparse graph appropriate for an edge list

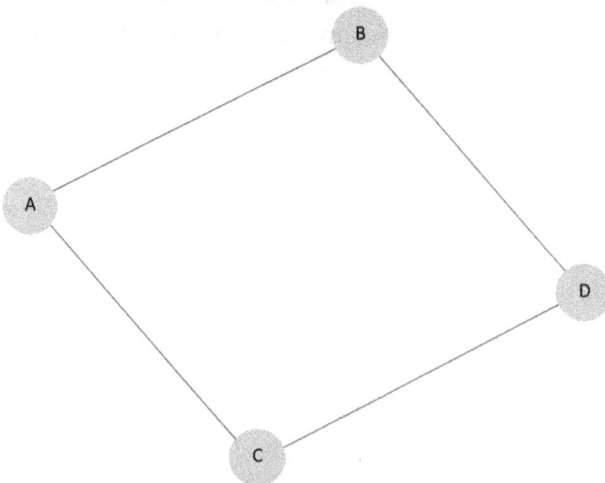

Graphs are widely used in real-life applications. We've already seen a few such as social networks and navigation, but they can also be used to map out connections for web crawling and for software package management, such as PIP. Now that we know the basic terminology, we can look at different forms of graphs.

8.2 Types of Graphs

Graphs come in distinct forms. Depending on the task at hand we may favor one type over the other. We subdivide graphs by looking at if they are directed or undirected, weighted or unweighted, cyclic or acyclic, and connected or disconnected. These properties can help tailor graphs to the specific task at hand.

8.2.1 Directed and Undirected Graphs

As we previously noted, graphs can either be directed or undirected. In an undirected graph, edges have no direction. Another way to look at this is that connections between nodes automatically connect both ways. We say the edge is bidirectional. In the early days of social media, connected members were both connected to each other in a friending system. If Aimee friended Brenda, Brenda also friended Aimee. The mutual connection was implied. In this case we do not include arrows on our graphs. In a directed graph, sometimes called a digraph, we have to indicate the direction of the edge. We can still have bidirectional edges, but it is no longer implied. Most modern social media platforms now operate on a following system so a bidirectional connection is not ensured. In this case we need to track the direction of the connection, although it certainly can be bidirectional.

8.2.2 Weighted and Unweighted Graphs

We also looked at weights in our introduction. An unweighted graph treats all edges as equal. We do not need to assign a value, although we often track the connection by assigning a value of one. Weighted graphs have value assigned to the connection and can represent positive or negative consequences depending on the situation. Commonly we assign weights based on cost, distance, or time to determine an optimal path. We could have a graph which represented the time to travel between points, or another which recorded the amount of gas burned traveling between them.

8.2.3 Cyclic and Acyclic Graphs

Most of the example graphs that we've seen in this chapter are cyclic graphs. A cyclic graph has at least one way that you can start on a node and find your way back to the same node. Figure 8.7 shows an acyclic graph of the design process on the left and a cyclic version of the same graph on the right. In the acyclic version, you can never get back to an earlier node. In the cyclic version if you start at the design phrase, you can find your back.

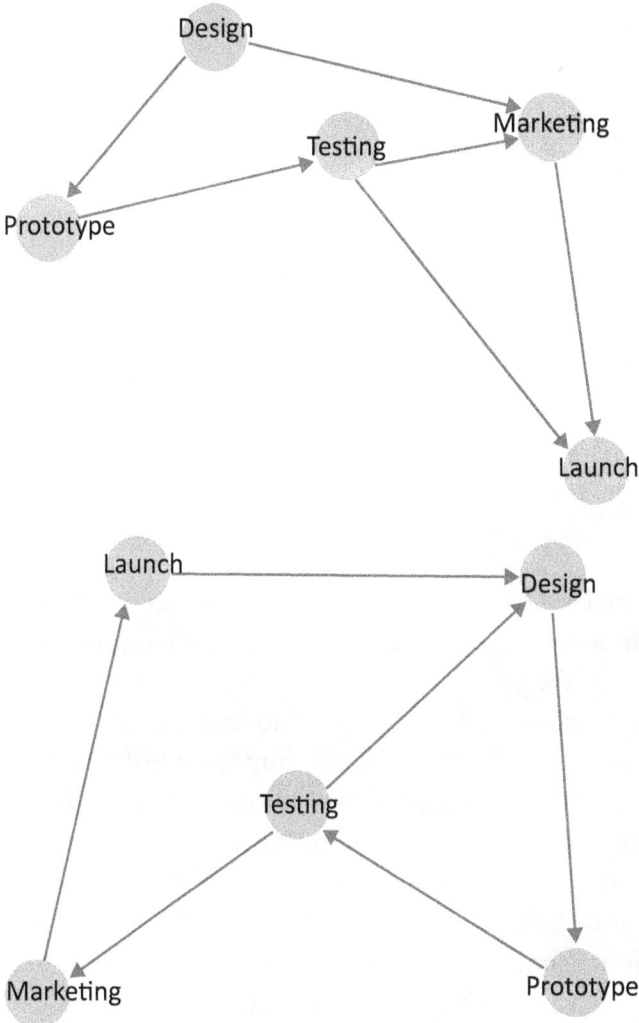

Figure 8.7 The design process in acyclic and cyclic forms

8.2.4 Connected and Disconnected Graphs

All of the examples that we have looked at up to this point
are connected graphs. This means that there are no isolated
nodes and that we can move from any node to any

other node, allowing for intermediate steps. If there is anode that cannot connect to any other particular node, then the graph is disconnected. Figure 8.8 shows a simple comparison between a connected graph and disconnected graph.

Figure 8.8   **A connected and disconnected graph**

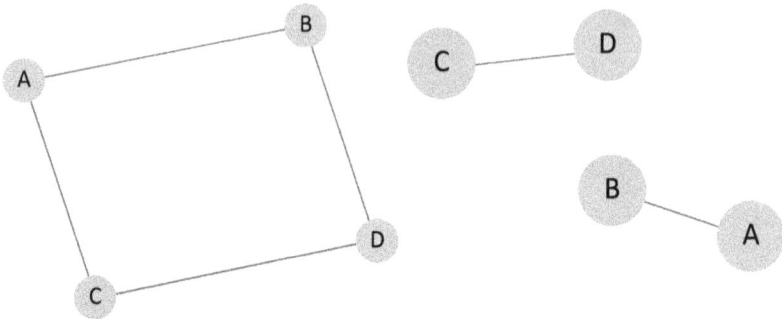

In the case of directed graphs, connectedness is a little trickier. Many directed graphs, due to the singular direction of some of the edges, do not fit our definition of connected. Figure 8.9 shows what is referred to as a weakly connected graph and a strongly connected graph. A weakly connected graph means that the nodes are all connected, but based on the direction of the edges we can't reach each node from every other node. In the weakly connected graph, we cannot reach node C from node A since the direction of the edge from B to C only runs one way. In a strongly connected graph, we can reach every node from every other node, like our undirected connected graphs.

Figure 8.9   A weakly connected and strongly connected graph

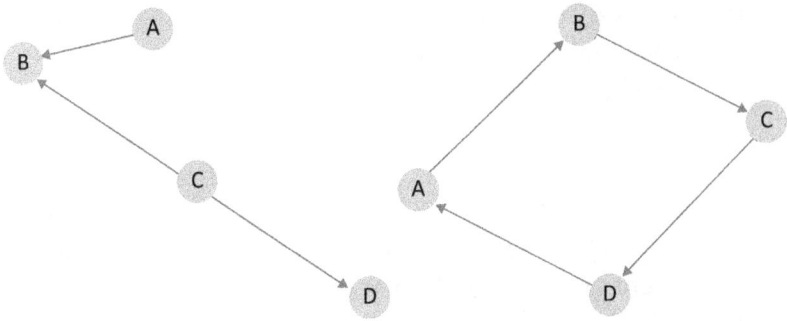

To determine the connectedness of a directed graph, the first task is to see if it would be connected without the directions on the edges. If not it is a disconnected graph. If we then consider the directions and we can still reach all of the nodes, then it is a strongly connected graph, otherwise it is a weakly connected graph.

8.3   Implementing Graphs

8.3.1 Trees as a Special Case of Graphs

Graphs can be a complex format to understand without a full understanding of the underlying concepts. Luckily we can draw from our experiences with trees to help us understand and implement graphs. Trees are a specific case of graphs and can be analyzed as such. Considering our types of graphs, trees are directed graphs. The relationship flows from the root down into the child nodes, but not backward. They are also weakly connected. All nodes are connected, but the directions of the edges prevent us from reaching them all. Trees are also acyclic, since we never loop back to earlier nodes. The trees we looked at were not weighted, although weighted trees can be used.

As such, the underlying code for graphs will share some similarities to trees, but will have some necessary differences. In fact, once we write our graph class, we could use it to create trees although our tree class will contain more specific methods towards trees.

8.3.2 The Graph Class

We have some important choices to make regarding how to implement our graphs. For versatility we will write the class to allow for graphs to be directed or undirected and to have weights if needed. For storing connections, we will use an adjacency list, since they are optimal in many cases.

We have a method for adding nodes, which only adds the node to the adjacency list if it is not already there. Unlike with trees and linked lists, we will not bother with a node class. The add_node() method is not meant to be called on its own, but is called when we add a new edge to ensure the nodes are set up. Once we add the edge, we check to see if it is a directed graph to see if we should also add the opposite connection.

To make things easier, we will also add a get_neighbors() method to get the adjacency list. This will return the list or a blank list if it has no neighbors.

```
class Graph:
    """
    Graph data structure using an
    adjacency list representation.
    """

    def __init__(self, directed=False):
        """
```

```
    Initialize the graph.
    Set directed=True for a directed graph.
    """
    self.adj_list = {}
    self.directed = directed

def add_node(self, node):
    """
    Add a node to the graph if it
    doesn't already exist.
    """
    if node not in self.adj_list:
      self.adj_list[node] = []

def add_edge(self, node1, node2, weight=1):
    """
    Add an edge from node1 to node2 with
    an optional weight (default = 1).
    """
    self.add_node(node1)
    self.add_node(node2)
    self.adj_list[node1].append((node2, weight))
    if not self.directed:
      self.adj_list[node2].append((node1, weight))

def get_neighbors(self, node):
    """
    Return a list of neighbors for the given node.
    """
    return self.adj_list.get(node, [])
```

To use our Graph class to create the directed graph seen in Figure 8.10 we use the code:

```
graph = Graph(directed=True)
graph.add_edge("A", "B")
graph.add_edge("A", "C")
graph.add_edge("B", "D")
graph.add_edge("C", "D")
```

Figure 8.10 **A sample graph**

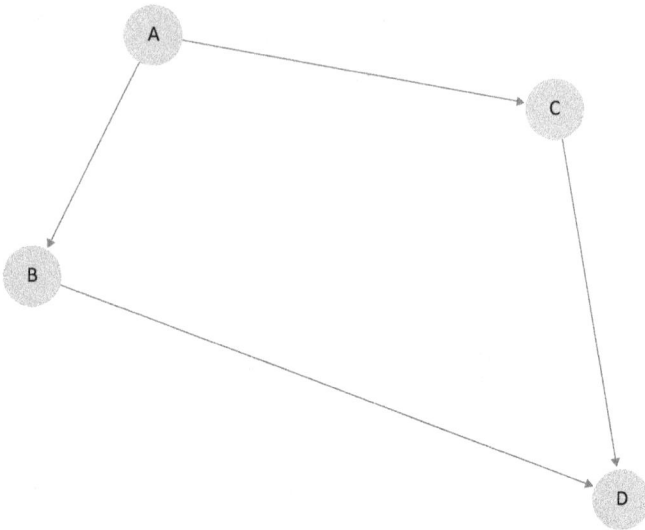

8.4   Graph Based Algorithms

8.4.1 Depth-First Search (DFS) and Breadth-First Search (BFS)

Like trees, we need to be able to traverse through our graphs to collect information and again we have the option of Depth-First or Breadth-First Search. We'll implement these as functions to allow us to choose between them based on our needs. The basic concept is the same as with trees, however since there can be cycles, we need to track the nodes which are visited to avoid endless looping.

For DFS, we use recursion to navigate to the furthest node away, avoiding any visited nodes.

```
def dfs(graph, start, visited=None):
    if visited is None:
        visited = set()
    visited.add(start)
    print(start, end=' ')
    for neighbor, _ in graph.get_neighbors(start):
        if neighbor not in visited:
            dfs(graph, neighbor, visited)
```

Using Figure 8.11 as an example and starting at A, we navigate from A to B and to D. Once we reach the end we backtrack to B, which has no further connections, so we backtrack to A. The next neighbor for A is C, which also leads us to E. This gives us A → B → D → C → E as our traversal.

Figure 8.11 **A sample graph for traversal**

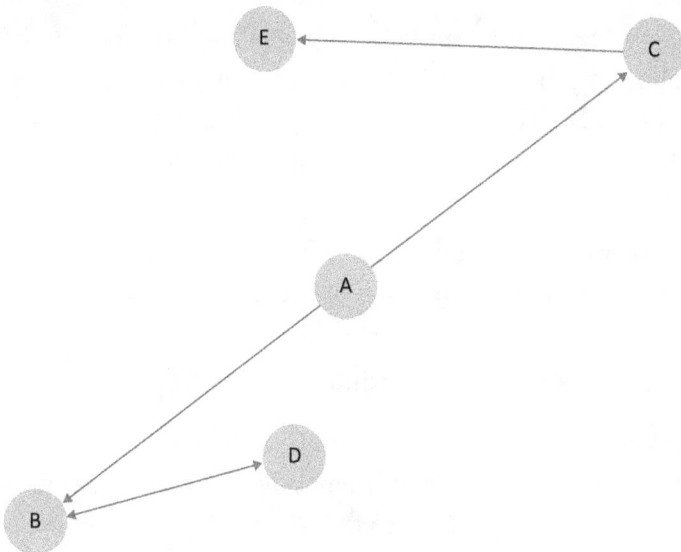

For breadth first search we can use our custom queue structure to ensure we visit all nodes at the first level before moving to the next. We add all of the neighbors from our starting node to the queue and then remove the first one, and add in all of its neighbors, excluding any previously visited nodes.

```
def bfs(graph, start):
    visited = set()
    queue = Queue()
    queue.enqueue(start)
    visited.add(start)

    while not queue.is_empty():
        node = queue.dequeue()
        print(node, end=' ')
        for neighbor, _ in graph.get_neighbors(node):
            if neighbor not in visited:
                visited.add(neighbor)
                queue.enqueue(neighbor)
```

Using Figure 8.11, and starting at A, we enqueue B and C. Following the first-in first out principle, we dequeue B and add in D. C is dequeued and E added. This just leaves D and E to be dequeued. This gives us the traversal A → B → C → D → E.

Knowing the different methods of traversal will serve us well as we implement other graph-based algorithms.

8.4.2 Dijkstra's Algorithm (Shortest Paths)

Dijkstra's algorithm is used to find the shortest path in a weighted graph. We start with a node and then expand out to the next unvisited node with the lowest distance, represented by the weight. This algorithm updates the distances as it goes to optimize the paths.

Since the algorithm simply chooses the nearest unvisited neighbor without checking other possibilities it is fairly efficient. This type of algorithm is known as a greedy algorithm, which we will explore in more detail in the next chapter.

Let's say we wanted to go from Chicago to Atlanta. Based on the graph seen in Figure 8.12, we can see that there are multiple paths we can take. Even in this simple example, we can see that there are multiple paths that we could take, but just imagine we were actually building a navigation app. We would need a very efficient algorithm.

Figure 8.12   Cities with distances

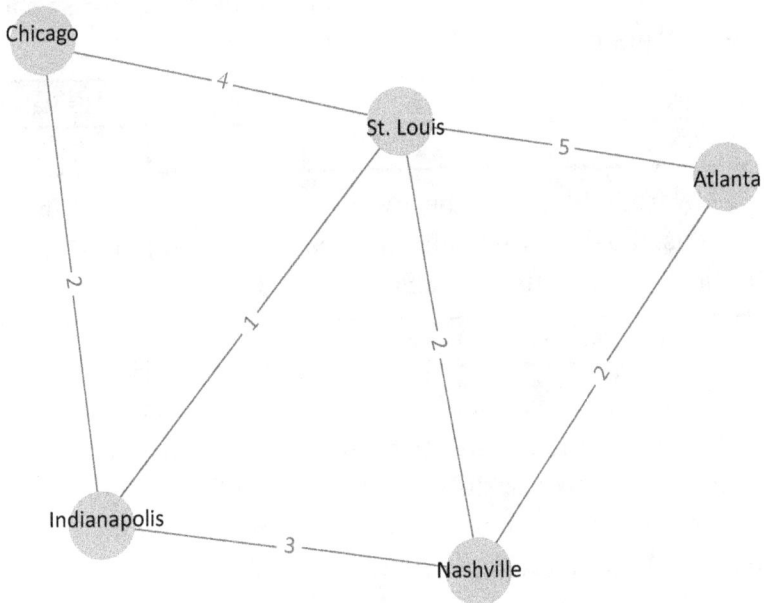

The goal is to record the shortest distance from Chicago, in this case, to every other city. We'll start by assuming that each city is infinitely far away and replace it with the shortest possible value as we see it. Since Chicago is our starting point, it has a distance of 0. From Chicago, we can directly reach St. Louis and Indianapolis, so we update their distances, based on the 0 at Chicago plus the weight on the connecting edge, so Indianapolis has a value of 2 and St. Louis has a value of 4.

Chicago	Indianapolis	St. Louis	Nashville	Atlanta
0	2	4	Infinity	Infinity

Since we have fully explored Chicago's neighbor's, we move to the lowest unexplored city, which would be Indianapolis. We add the 2 we know it takes to get to Indianapolis to the edge weights of its unexplored neighbors. Via Indianapolis, it only takes 3 to get to St. Louis, which is better than the 4 directly from Chicago, so we update that value. Nashville is 3 from Indianapolis, plus the 2, gives us a best distance of 5.

Chicago	Indianapolis	St. Louis	Nashville	Atlanta
0	2	3	5	Infinity

Onward to St. Louis, the lowest unexplored vertex. Via St. Louis, the distance to Nashville is 5. No need to update a duplicate value. Atlanta via St. Louis is 8, so that is updated.

Chicago	Indianapolis	St. Louis	Nashville	Atlanta
0	2	3	5	8

We have found a distance to Atlanta, but we can't be sure yet if it is the shortest distance since currently Nashville is the next city to explore. Via Nashville, we have another 2 to get to Atlanta, giving us a distance of 7, better than our current 8.

Chicago	Indianapolis	St. Louis	Nashville	Atlanta
0	2	3	5	7

Since Atlanta is our smallest unexplored city, and also our target, we have found that the shortest distance is 7.

In code, we use a dictionary for quick lookup, starting with infinity for everything except the starting city, which is 0. We use an empty set to track explored vertices. Typically in Dijkstra's algorithm we explore every connected node, so we use a while loop to determine when we have successfully completed the algorithm. As explained above, we add the edge weights to update the values and then assign the closest to the `current_node` before continuing.

```
def dijkstra(graph, start):
    distances = {
        node: float('inf') for node in graph.adj_list
        }
    distances[start] = 0
    visited = set()

    while len(visited) < len(graph.adj_list):
        # Find the unvisited node with
        # the smallest distance
        current_node = None
        current_distance = float('inf')
        for node in graph.adj_list:
            if (node not in visited
                and distances[node] < current_distance
                ):
                current_node = node
                current_distance = distances[node]

        if current_node is None:
            break
```

```
visited.add(current_node)

for neighbor, weight in (
  graph.get_neighbors(current_node)
  ):
  if neighbor not in visited:
    distance = current_distance + weight
    if distance < distances[neighbor]:
      distances[neighbor] = distance


return distances
```

It is worth noting that Dijkstra's algorithm does not return the shortest path, but rather the length of the shortest path. In fact, it gives us the shortest distance to each node, not just the target. Note as well, that the edge weight could be representative of other values as well. We could be considered with time, fuel efficiency, tourist locations, or any other number of factors.

In terms of complexity, the time complexity is $O(V^2)$ since we visit each vertex and then update all vertices from there. The space complexity is $O(V)$ since we need to store information about each vertex.

8.4.3 A* (A Star)

If you have a basic knowledge of American geography, you may have noticed that in our city graphs we have not been placing our cities with any real world accuracy. This is fine since graphs are only concerned with the connected, and optionally the weights. A*, pronounced A star, takes additional information into account. Instead of blindly jumping to vertice based closest to the starting city, we can use an educated guess to move us in the correct direction. Looking at Figure 8.13, it is no wonder that moving through St. Louis on our way to Atlanta was not a reasonable choice. Using our knowledge of the world we can avoid vertices which are obviously not the best choice, therefore improving the speed of our algorithm.

Figure 8.13 A graph of cities based on physical location

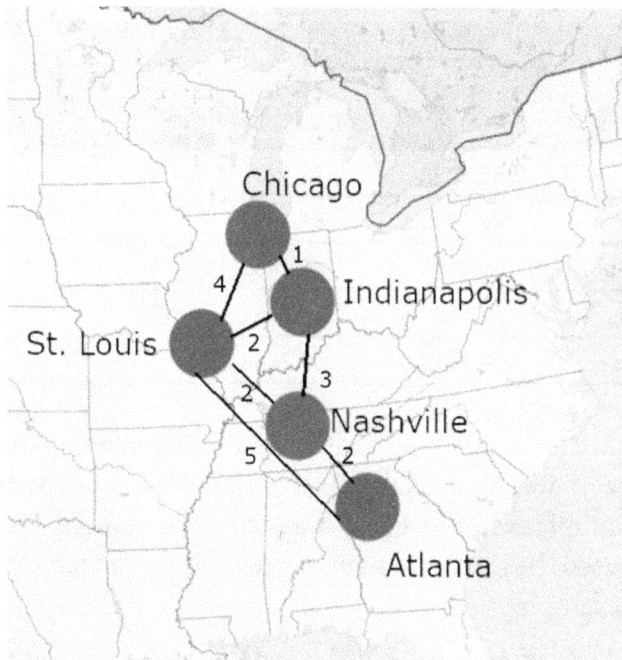

Like most improvements there is a drawback here as well. We now have the task of giving the computer some real world information to help aid the algorithm. This will allow the algorithm to guess the correct path and ignore likely incorrect paths. In some cases this estimate can be difficult to determine, but in our case we can use the latitude and longitude of the cities to calculate the distance based on the Pythagorean theorem. This won't give us the exact distance by road, but is a reasonable estimate. The method by which we determine this estimate is called a heuristic and is a critical step in our algorithm. Incorrect heuristics will send A* down the wrong path, wasting time. Table 8.1 shows the latitude and longitude of the cities we will use.

Table 8.1	GPS data from SimpleMaps, along with additional calculation[8]		
City	Latitude	Longitude	Calculated distance from Atlanta (rounded)
Atlanta	33.7628	-84.422	0
Chicago	41.8375	-87.6866	9
Indianapolis	39.7771	-86.1458	6
St. Louis	38.6359	-90.2451	8
Nashville	36.1715	-86.7842	3

While this is not an accurate way to calculate the actual distance, it does give us values that are in the range with our simple graph example. For more accurate distances, GeoPy can be used, however these values would not match up for us in this example[9].

The logic of A* starts out similarly to Dijkstra's Algorithm, but we also need to keep track of our estimated remaining distance. Traditionally we use "f" for the total estimated cost, "g" for actual cost from the start, and "h" for the estimated cost to the end, however we will use more descriptive language. We will also track the previous nodes so that we can report the optimal path as well.

8. SimpleMaps, *U.S. Cities Database*, accessed April 6, 2025, https://simplemaps.com/data/us-cities.
9. geopy 2.4.1 Documentation, accessed April 6, 2025, https://geopy.readthedocs.io/en/stable/#

We start in Chicago and explore its neighbors. It takes 1 to get to Indianapolis and we estimate that Atlanta is 6 away, so the estimate via Atlanta is 7. Via St. Louis, we get an estimate of 12: 4 for the edge plus 8 for the estimate. This is the power of A*, since we now know that St. Louis is likely not a reasonable city to route through and can likely be ignored. So we move on to Indianapolis.

	Cost So Far	Estimated Cost to Goal	Total Estimated Cost	Came From
Chicago	0	9	9	None
Indianapolis	1	6	7	Chicago
St. Louis	4	8	12	Chicago
Nashville		3		
Atlanta		0		

Exploring from Indianapolis, we look at the cost to its neighbors, Nashville and St. Louis. Keeping in mind that we have already travelled 1, we add that to the edge costs. This gives us 4 to Nashville (1 + 3) plus the remaining estimate of 3, giving a total of 7. St. Louis via Indianapolis would also be 3 (1 + 2). Since this is better, we update the values with an estimate of 11 (3 + 8). Nashville is the best choice now, so we continue to ignore St. Louis.

	Cost So Far	Estimated Cost to Goal	Total Estimated Cost	Came From
Chicago	0	9	9	None
Indianapolis	1	6	8	Chicago
St. Louis	4 3	8	12 11	Indianapolis
Nashville	4	3	7	Indianapolis
Atlanta		0		

From Nashville we visit St. Louis with a cost of 6 (4 + 2). Since this is worse than the route via Indianapolis, we do not update any values. Atlanta, our target, is next. We get a travelled distance of 6 (4+2) and we will also update the estimate to 6.

	Cost So Far	Estimated Cost to Goal	Total Estimated Cost	Came From
Chicago	0	9	9	None
Indianapolis	2	6	8	Chicago
St. Louis	~~4~~ 3	8	~~12~~ 11	Indianapolis
Nashville	4	3	7	Indianapolis
Atlanta	6	0	6	Nashville

Since we have reached Atlanta by exploring the optimal path, there is no need to search any further. This is, of course, dependent on how accurate our heuristic is at providing the estimate, so we have to put more thought into implementation of the algorithm. That up front work may take a little longer, but has no impact on the time and space complexity and is a worthy tradeoff. We can also determine the path we took by tracking back through the path. Atlanta was visited from Nashville, which was visited from Indianapolis. Indianapolis was visited from Chicago. Reversing this list we get the optimal path Chicago, Indianapolis, Nashville, Atlanta.

In code we have a few choices to make. First we will calculate the straight line distance between cities rather than supplying it. This is so we could update the heuristic if we needed to improve our estimates.

```
from math import sqrt

#Heuristic: straight-line distance
#between two cities

def estimate_distance(city1, city2, gps_coords):
  lat1, lon1 = gps_coords[city1]
  lat2, lon2 = gps_coords[city2]
  return sqrt((lat1 - lat2)**2 + (lon1 - lon2)**2)
```

Second, we need to determine a way of storing our information. Dictionaries are a great choice for quick lookups. We will initialize everything with a distance of infinity and update as we traverse. Our estimates and totals to date will also be stored in separate dictionaries. We could use a dictionary of dictionaries, however this would complicate the code and for small examples will not make a major difference. We will also store our path in a separate dictionary. This does increase the space complexity of our algorithm, but saves time by not having to rebuild the path on a second pass through.

```
# A* search using a graph object
# and external GPS coords
def a_star(graph, gps_coords, start, goal):
  # Initialize cost dictionaries
  cost_so_far = {
    node: float('inf') for node in graph.adj_list
    }
  cost_so_far[start] = 0
```

```
total_estimated_cost = {
  node: float('inf') for node in graph.adj_list
  }
total_estimated_cost[start] = estimate_distance(
  start, goal, gps_coords
  )

visited = set()
came_from = {}

while len(visited) < len(graph.adj_list):
  # Find unvisited city with the lowest
  # estimated total cost
  current_city = None
  current_cost = float('inf')
  for city in graph.adj_list:
      if city in visited:
          Continue
  est_cost = total_estimated_cost[city]
  if est_cost < current_cost
      current_city = city
      current_cost = est_cost

  if (
    current_city is None
    or current_city == goal
    ):
    break

  visited.add(current_city)
```

```
    for neighbor, edge_weight in (
      graph.get_neighbors(current_city)
    ):
      if neighbor in visited:
        continue

    new_cost = (
      cost_so_far[current_city] + edge_weight
      )
    if new_cost < cost_so_far[neighbor]:
      came_from[neighbor] = current_city
      cost_so_far[neighbor] = new_cost
      total_estimated_cost[neighbor] = (
        new_cost + estimate_distance(
          neighbor, goal, gps_coords
          )
        )

# Reconstruct path
path = []
current = goal
if current in came_from or current == start:
  while current in came_from:
    path.append(current)
    current = came_from[current]
  path.append(start)
  path.reverse()
  return path, cost_so_far[goal]
else:
  return None, float('inf')
```

Our time complexity would have a worse case of $O(V^2)$ since we look at all unvisited nodes for each node we visit, however it is worth noting that with a well designed heuristic, we ideally should not be visiting each node. The space complexity would be $O(V)$ since we need to store information on each node. It may feel as though this is a low estimate since we are storing the cost so far, total estimated cost, previous nodes, and visited nodes, however this will only grow linearly as the number of vertices increases.

8.4.4 Floyd-Warshall Algorithm

Floyd-Warshall is another common path-finding algorithm with graphs. It determines the shortest paths between all pairs of vertices. In many situations this makes it less efficient than Dijkstar's or A*. However, there are times where it is extremely useful. First, we may need all of the paths, which would require our previous algorithms to be run multiple times. Second, Floyd-Warshall can reliably handle negative weights which can cause incorrect results in our other algorithms.

The concept of a negative edge weight can be tricky to understand, however there are many places where we could need them. For example if we were working with shipping routes, there could be government incentives or rebates which could lead to some paths having a negative cost, or rather a profit. When determining the most cost efficient route, we would need to take this into account.

For our example, we will look at the carbon cost of moving throughout a city. Most routes will be major roadways, having a positive carbon cost, but we can also have carbon negative routes like subways or electric buses. Figure 8.14 shows the layout of our city transportation network. Floyd-Warshall assumes that a graph is directed, so we will have a one-way traffic setup in our city to simplify the example.

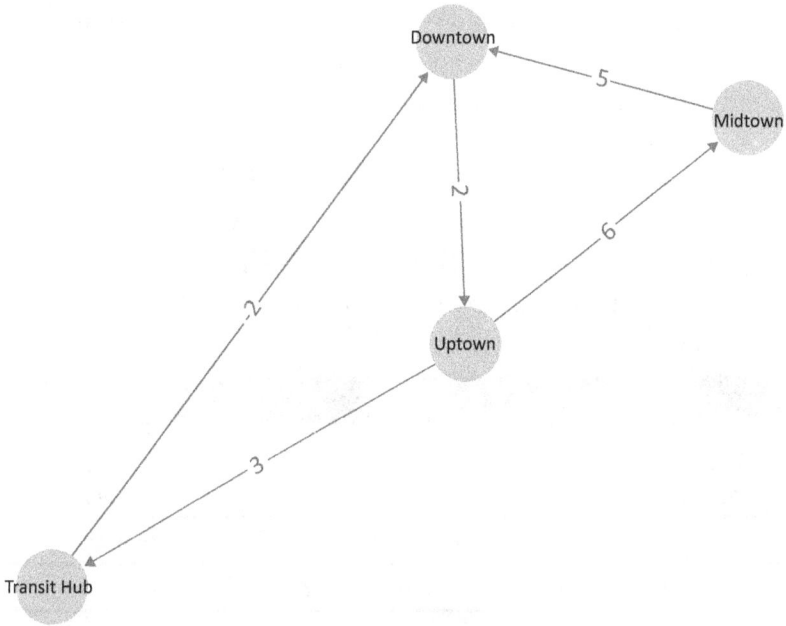

Figure 8.14 Carbon costs of moving about a one-way transportation network

We record our information within a 2 dimensional table which contains the lowest carbon cost. The main diagonal will be 0 as it costs nothing to stay in place. Any known edges will be recorded and everything else will have an starting cost of infinity.

	Uptown	Midtown	Downtown	Transit Hub
Uptown	0	6	Infinity	3
Midtown	Infinity	0	5	Infinity
Downtown	2	Infinity	0	Infinity
Transit Hub	Infinity	Infinity	-2	0

Here's where Floyd-Warshall gets a little inefficient. We have to use each vertex as an intermediate node to see if we can find more efficient paths. Starting with Uptown, we check each pair, routing it through Uptown to see if there is an improvement, looking up the values in the table. We can skip the ones that already start at Uptown and focus on the rest. Routing from Midtown through Uptown will not result in any improvement, since we currently have Midtown to Uptown as an infinite cost. Downtown already goes directly to Uptown, but there are no paths that do not have an infinite cost being added in. This is likewise true for the Transit Hub. Downtown can get to Uptown with a cost of 2, so we need to look at that a little closer. Downtown → Uptown → Midtown has a total cost of 8 (2 + 6) while Downtown → Uptown → Transit Hub has a cost of 5 (2 + 3).

	Uptown	Midtown	Downtown	Transit Hub
Uptown	0	6	Infinity	3
Midtown	Infinity	0	5	Infinity
Downtown	2	~~Infinity~~ 8	0	~~Infinity~~ 5
Transit Hub	Infinity	Infinity	-2	0

Next we route through Midtown. Uptown to Midtown is 6, so we can update our cost to Downtown to 11 (6 + 5) since it is less than infinity. Downtown to Midtown is 8, but there are no better routes to be found from there. The transit hub has infinite cost to Midtown, so we ignore it.

	Uptown	Midtown	Downtown	Transit Hub
Uptown	0	6	~~Infinity~~ 11	3
Midtown	Infinity	0	5	Infinity
Downtown	2	~~Infinity~~ 8	0	~~Infinity~~ 5
Transit Hub	Infinity	Infinity	-2	0

Let's consider Downtown as the intermediate point. Uptown to Downtown is 11, so that route to Midtown gives 17 and to the Transit Hub gives 14, so no updates required. Midtown to Downtown is 5 and Downtown to Uptown is 2, so Midtown to Uptown is now 7 (5 + 2). Downtown to the Transit Hub is 5, so Midtown to the Transit Hub is now 10 (5 + 5). Considering the Transit Hub to Downtown we start with a cost of -2. This gives us a few updates. The Transit Hub to Uptown is now 0 (-2 + 2) and to Midtown is 6 (-2 + 8).

	Uptown	Midtown	Downtown	Transit Hub
Uptown	0	6	~~Infinity~~ 11	3
Midtown	~~Infinity~~ 7	0	5	~~Infinity~~ 10
Downtown	2	~~Infinity~~ 8	0	~~Infinity~~ 5
Transit Hub	~~Infinity~~ 0	~~Infinity~~ 6	-2	0

Finally, we need to route through the Transit Hub. Uptown to the Hub is 3, so we can get to Midtown we 9 (3 + 6), but since we already have a cost of 6 we ignore this. Downtown can be reached for 1 (3 + -2) which is a vast improvement over 11. Midtown to the Hub is 10 and yields no improvements. Likewise Downtown yields no improvements with the initial distance of 5.

	Uptown	Midtown	Downtown	Transit Hub
Uptown	0	6	~~Infinity 11~~ 1	3
Midtown	~~Infinity~~ 7	0	5	~~Infinity~~ 10
Downtown	2	~~Infinity~~ 8	0	~~Infinity~~ 5
Transit Hub	~~Infinity~~ 0	~~Infinity~~ 6	-2	0

The code for Floyd Warshall follows the logic already explained. We create a dictionary of dictionaries to store all of the costs. A two dimensional array is also a good choice for storing costs if numerical keys are being used. We start with everything at infinity and set the zeroes and known edge weights.

After that, it is a matter of going through the intermediate nodes and checking to see if any improvements are found.

```
def floyd_warshall(graph):
  nodes = list(graph.adj_list.keys())

  # Initialize the cost dictionary
  cost = {
    from_node: {
      to_node: float('inf') for to_node in nodes
    }
    for from_node in nodes
  }

  # Set initial costs from graph edges
  for node in nodes:
    cost[node][node] = 0  # cost to self is zero
    for neighbor, weight in (
      graph.get_neighbors(node)
      ):
      cost[node][neighbor] = weight

  # Main Floyd-Warshall loop
  for intermediate in nodes:
    for start in nodes:
      for end in nodes:
        new_cost = (
          cost[start][intermediate]
          + cost[intermediate][end]
        )
        if cost[start][end] > new_cost:
          cost[start][end] = new_cost

  return cost
```

The triple for loop gives us a time complexity of $O(V^3)$, so this algorithm should only be used if it is the best fit for a problem. Even optimizing to skip loops whenever we find an infinite cost, there will be minimal improvement as it is still running in cubic time for large inputs. The space complexity is $O(V^2)$ since we are storing the cost for each pair of vertices.

The algorithms we've explored in this section have similar uses, but there is no clear winner here. It is important to consider the specific needs of our problem and choose the best algorithm for the situation. By understanding a multitude of ways to approach similar problems, we can build our skills as programmers and approach problems in an efficient manner.

8.5 Practical Application - Longest Influence Chain

We've already looked at how a social network can be modelled using a graph. Users can be represented as nodes and connections can be represented by directed edges that show who follows whom. For marketing purposes, we may want to find the user with the longest chain of influence to sponsor. Investing in a long chain of influence could reach more users than just finding the person with the greatest number of followers.

Once we construct our graph, we can loop through each user and perform a depth-first search to explore all possible chains starting from that user. We can keep track of the longest chain per user and compare them once we have finished looping through all of the users. For simplicity, we are going to assume that the graph is acyclic.

We'll modify our earlier dfs function to return the length of the path rather than printing out the nodes. We return `1 + max_length` to account for the user themselves in the count.

```
def dfs_longest_chain(graph, node, visited):
  visited.add(node)
  max_length = 0
  for neighbor, _ in graph.get_neighbors(node):
    if neighbor not in visited:
      length = dfs_longest_chain(
        graph, neighbor, visited
        )
      max_length = max(max_length, length)
  # backtrack after exploration
  visited.remove(node)
  return 1 + max_length
```

To find the longest chain, we loop through the users, run our dfs_longest_chain function and return the user with the longest chain and the length of their chain.

```
def find_longest_influence_chain(graph):
  longest_user = None
  longest_chain = 0

  for user in graph.adj_list:
    visited = set()
    chain_length = dfs_longest_chain(
      graph, user, visited
      )
    if chain_length > longest_chain:
      longest_chain = chain_length
      longest_user = user

  return longest_user, longest_chain
```

Figure 8.15 shows a sample social network to explore.

Figure 8.15 Social network

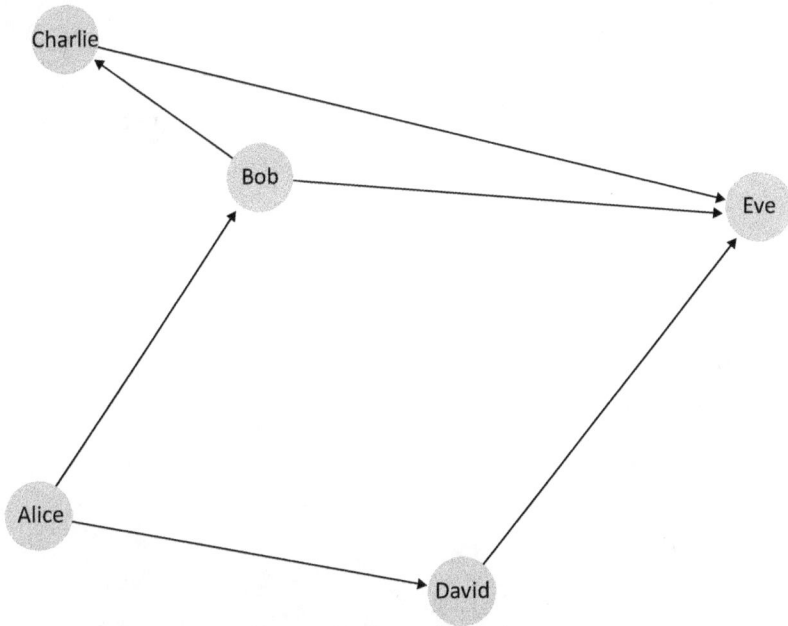

```
g = Graph(directed=True)
g.add_edge('Alice', 'Bob')
g.add_edge('Alice', 'David')
g.add_edge('Bob', 'Charlie')
g.add_edge('Bob', 'Eve')
g.add_edge('Charlie', 'Eve')
g.add_edge('David', 'Eve')

user, chain = find_longest_influence_chain(g)
print(f"User with the longest chain: {user}")
print(f"Length of longest chain: {chain}")
```

This example shows that Alice would be the ideal candidate for the sponsorship with a longest length of 4.

Each DFS could take up to $O(V + E)$ and since we need to do one more each node, the total time complexity is $O(V \times (V+E))$. This would be extremely slow for dense graphs. We'll revisit this next chapter to improve on the efficiency. The space complexity is $O(V)$ due to the recursion stack and the visited set.

Chapter Summary

- Graphs are collections of nodes connected by edges, used to model networks, relationships, and paths.

- Graphs can be directed, weighted, cyclic, or disconnected.

- Graphs can be represented as adjacency lists, matrices, or edge lists.

- Graphs can be traversed by BFS and DFS.

- Many algorithms have been developed to find the shortest path in graphs, such as Dijkstra's Algorithm, A*, and Floyd-Warshall.

Quiz

1. **What is the term of a node in a graph?**
   a. Edge
   b. Leaf
   c. Path
   d. Vertex

2. **Which describes a directed graph?**
   a. All weights are positive
   b. Edges connect every pair of vertices
   c. Edges have a direction from one vertex to another
   d. It cannot contain cycles

3. **Which graph representation is most memory efficient for sparse graphs?**
   a. Adjacency matrix
   b. Adjacency list
   c. Edge matrix
   d. Tree list

4. **What makes a graph cyclic?**
   a. All nodes are connected
   b. It contains a loop where a path returns to the same node
   c. It contains only directed edges
   d. It has a node with more than two edges

5. **In an unweighted graph, what does BFS find?**

   a. Cycles
   b. The longest path
   c. The path with the highest weight
   d. The path is the fewest edges

6. **What is a key requirement for using Dijkstra's algorithm?**

   a. Graph must be directed
   b. Graph must be fully connected
   c. Graph must have non-negative weights
   d. Heuristics must be defined

7. **How is A* different from Dijkstra's Algorithm?**

   a. It always finds the longest path
   b. It uses a heuristic to estimate the distance to the goal
   c. It uses recursion instead of iteration
   d. It works only on unweighted graphs

8. **Which algorithm finds the shortest paths between all pairs of vertices?**

   a. A*
   b. BFS
   c. Dijkstra
   d. Floyd-Warshal

9. **What does a heuristic function provide in A*?**

   a. A limit on the number of visited nodes
   b. An estimate of remaining cost to the goal
   c. The exact path to the goal
   d. The total number of hops

10. Which algorithm works best for finding the shortest path in a graph with negative edge weights?

   a. A*
   b. BFS
   c. Dijkstra
   d. Floyd-Warshal

Answers

1 – d	2 – c	3 – b	4 – b	5 – d
6 – c	7 – b	8 – d	9 – b	10 – d

CHAPTER 9

Dynamic Programming and Greedy Algorithms

Key Learning Objectives

- Understand dynamic programming and how it optimizes solutions.
- Understand greedy algorithms and where they can be used.
- Explore memoization and tabulation: two dynamic programming techniques.
- Explore solutions to classic problems.

In this chapter, we introduce optimization techniques like dynamic programming and greedy algorithms. These do not rely on specific data structures and are a new method of looking at problems. We will look at some specific problems and learn about when these methods can and cannot be used.

9.1 Introduction to Dynamic Programming and Greedy Algorithms

Throughout this book, we have focused on specific data structures and the algorithms that complement them. Now, however, we will be looking at strategies. Dynamic programming (DP) is an approach to optimizing solutions by avoiding redundant work. It does so by breaking problems into subproblems and only solving them once. Greedy algorithms have been used in the graph chapter and work by choosing the best options for the moment and backtracking if needed. In this chapter, we will investigate greedy algorithms further and determine where they are useful and how they can fail.

9.1.1 What is Dynamic Programming?

Dynamic programming is best used when problems can be broken down into subproblems that overlap. This means the same computations are needed multiple times. We can then build the optimal solution by combining the solutions to the subproblems. Often, problems that use recursion repeat the same calculations repeatedly. If we store the solutions instead of repeating the calculation, we can ultimately save time, although at a space tradeoff.

Way back in Chapter 2, we looked at solving the fibonacci sequence recursively. The code is shown as a refresher.

```
def fibonacci_recursive(n):
    #base case
    if n <= 1:
        return n
    #recursive call
    return (
        fibonacci_recursive(n - 1)
        + fibonacci_recursive(n - 2)
    )
```

Figure 9.1 shows the recursive calls to solve for 5.

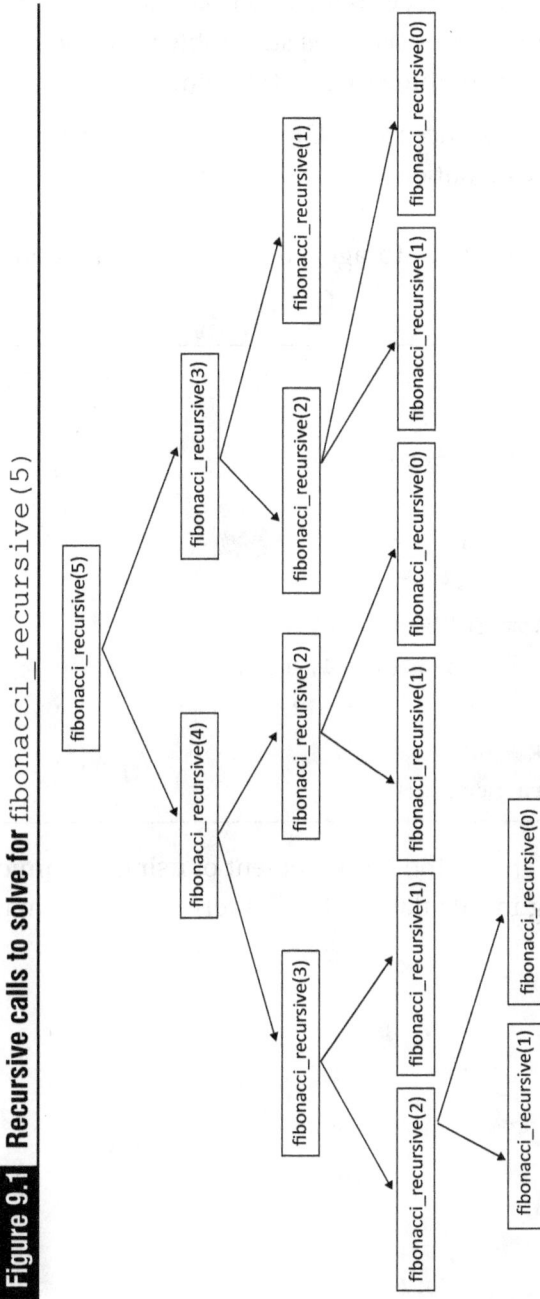

Figure 9.1 Recursive calls to solve for fibonacci_recursive(5)

What seemed like an optimal solution to us earlier certainly has a lot of repetition. This is an ideal place to use dynamic programming as it has subproblems and repeated calculations that combine to give the solution.

The main difference in the DP approach is storing the results of the calculations and looking them up without recursing if the same calculations would recur. We have many options for data storage, but we will use a dictionary for simplicity.

```python
def fib_dp(n, memo={}):
    if n in memo:
        return memo[n]
    if n <= 1:
        memo[n] = n
    else:
        memo[n] = (
            fib_dp(n - 1, memo)
            + fib_dp(n - 2, memo)
        )
    return memo[n]
```

Figure 9.2 shows the improvement of using dynamic programming in calculating the first term in the Fibonacci sequence.

| Figure 9.2 | **Recursive calls to solve for** fibonacci_dp(5) |

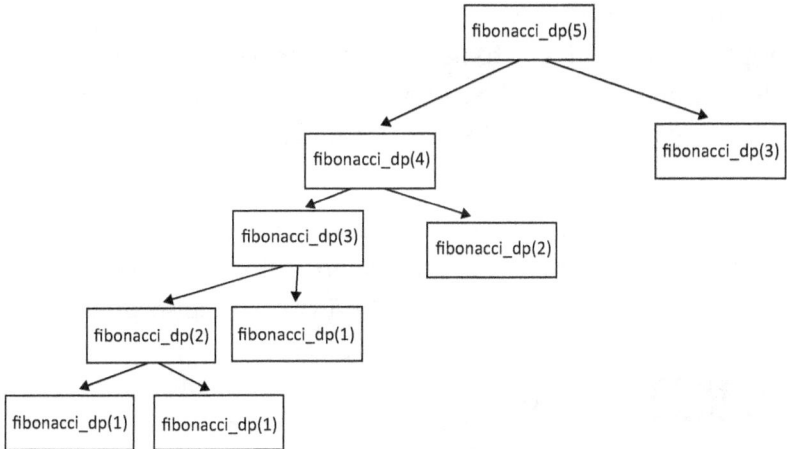

This simple change reduces the time complexity from $O(2^n)$ to $O(n)$ since each unique subproblem is only solved once. The overall space complexity is still $O(n)$ since the recursion stack is still as deep as the value entered; however, the overall number of function calls is significantly reduced. The extra storage to avoid the redundancy also grows linearly, so it has no impact on the algorithm's space complexity.

This particular DP technique is called memoization and involves calculating and storing results as we go. Tabulation, another DP technique, involves calculating the solutions of the subproblems first and can eliminate the recursion altogether. We will explore both methods in more detail later in the chapter.

9.1.2 What is a Greedy Algorithm?

Greedy algorithms make the best choice at each step, hoping that this leads to the best choice overall. Greedy algorithms are often simpler and faster; however, they may not always return the globally optimal solution.

To illustrate, imagine if we had six piles of coins, as in Figure 9.3. We are allowed to take any pile, but we cannot take two piles in a row. In other words, if we take the 5 coins in the first pile, we cannot take the 1 coin in the second pile.

Figure 9.3   Piles of coins

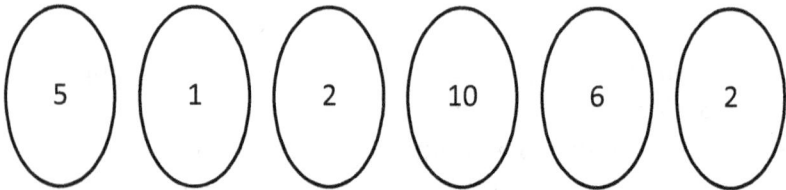

It shouldn't be hard for a person to realise that the most coins you can obtain is 17 by taking the 1st, 4th, and 6th piles, but coding this would be more difficult. Using brute force, we would need to loop multiple times, picking and skipping different values, but this would not be very efficient. We could try our new dynamic programming technique to track various combinations, but this would be challenging to code. Instead, a greedy approach can be attempted.

The logic would be to start at the beginning and to choose the highest of the first two. This ensures that we do not skip over a value higher than the coins we pick up. So we would take 5, since it is higher than 1. We skip 1 and choose between 2 and 10. Since 10 is higher, we take that. This makes us skip the 6. Only 2 is left, so we take that as well. In this case, we did get the optimal result of 17 (5 + 10 + 2), but this simple example does show some of the danger in the greedy approach. By only considering the locally best choice, we are ignoring possible benefits that we could miss out on later. Imagine if the fifth coin pile had 50 coins? Our current algorithm would miss it completely by choosing 10 over 2.

The code, however, is ridiculously simple and very efficient, so we need to consider whether the potential risk is worth it.

```
coins = [5, 1, 2, 10, 6]
i = 0
total = 0

while i < len(coins):
    if (
            i + 1 < len(coins)

            and coins[i+1] > coins[i]
            ):
            total += coins[i+1]
            i += 2
    else:
            total += coins[i]
            i += 2

print(total)
```

The time complexity of this algorithm is O(n) since we only need to take one loop through. We only track the total, so space complexity is O(1).

The decision whether to choose greedy algorithms depends on a few factors. The most important thing is that it follows the greedy-choice property. Will choosing the local optima always lead to the global optimum? If this is the case, greedy algorithms are amazing. There are also times when the greedy solution and the optimal solution are so similar that the time saving is worth a slight inaccuracy. We will explore this in later sections.

9.2 Greedy Algorithm Examples

Greedy algorithms are amazing when they work as expected. In situations where local optima leads to a globally optimal solution, greedy algorithms provide a quick and efficient solution to complex problems.

9.2.1 Activity Selection

The activity selection problem involves choosing the maximum number of activities possible without any overlap. The brute force method involves checking all subsets of the activities and reporting which would have the maximum length. This, however, would quickly become unmanageable as the number of activities increases.

The greedy approach is to always choose the activity that finishes earliest. This leaves maximal time for future activities. Table 9.1 shows university course offerings that a student needs to take, and they would like to complete as many as possible in their semester. For convenience, these are organized by end time.

Table 9.1 Fictional university course offerings

Class	Start Time	End Time
Calculus 1	8	9
Computer Science 1	10	11
Environmental Lab	9	12
Literature 1	11	12
Biology Lab	11	13
Physics Lab	13	15
Art 1	14	15

Once sorted, we start with the earliest ending class, Calculus 1. We check the next ending class, Computer Science 1, making sure it has not already started. Since it has not, we add it. Moving on, the Environmental Lab has already started, so we add Literature 1. Biology Lab is the next, but it has already started, but Physics Lab has not, so we add it. We will still be in the lab when Art 1 begins, so we are finished. So the maximum number of courses we can take is 4.

This approach will give the maximum number of courses in a single pass through the course offerings, giving us O(n log n) time complexity, due to the need for sorting first. For space, it depends on exactly what we intend to return. Returning just the number of courses would be O(1) while a course listing would be O(n) at worst.

```
def activity_selection(classes):
    # Sort classes by end time
    classes.sort(key=lambda x: x['end'])

    selected = []
    last_end = 0

    for cls in classes:
        if cls['start'] >= last_end:
            selected.append(cls)
            last_end = cls['end']

    return selected
```

9.2.2 Fractional Knapsack Problem

The fractional knapsack problem involves maximizing the value of items to be carried in a knapsack. There are variants of this problem, but this one allows fractions of items to be taken. A traditional brute force solution could involve looping over items to compare the total amount, but the fractional amounts would make it problematic and time-consuming. The greedy algorithm works by choosing items based on the value-to-weight ratio, focusing on the most valuable first. Since there are no restrictions on the fractions, the locally greedy choices will produce the optimal result.

As an example, consider a 50 kg capacity knapsack that can be filled with three different items. We have 10 kg of gold valued at 60K, 20 kg of silver valued at 100K, and 30 kg of copper valued at 90K. In our algorithm, regardless of the items, we must first determine the value per kg and then sort from highest to lowest. So we look at gold first (6), silver (5), and then copper (3).

Once sorted, we start at the first item and take as much as possible. If there is any capacity left, we move to the next item until there is no room left. In this particular example, we would take all of the gold, all of the silver, and 20 kg of the copper. This gives us 220 K (60 + 100 + ⅔ x 90), the optimal result.

```python
def fractional_knapsack(items, capacity):
  # Calculate value per kg for each item
  for item in items:
    item['value_per_kg'] = (
      item['value'] / item['weight']
    )

  # Sort by value per kg, descending
  items.sort(
    key=lambda x: x['value_per_kg'], reverse=True
    )

  total_value = 0
  result = []

  for item in items:
    if capacity == 0:
      break
```

```
    if item['weight'] <= capacity:
      # Take the whole item
      total_value += item['value']
      result.append({
        'item': item['name'],
        'taken': 1.0,
        'value_gained': item['value']
        })
      capacity -= item['weight']
    else:
      # Take a fraction of the item
      fraction = capacity / item['weight']
      value_gained = item['value'] * fraction
      total_value += value_gained
      result.append({
        'item': item['name'],
        'taken': round(fraction, 2),
        'value_gained': round(value_gained)
        })
      capacity = 0

  return total_value, result
```

This straightforward algorithm has a time complexity of O(n log n), mainly due to the sorting of the items. The space complexity is O(n) due to the storage of the results.

9.2.3 0/1 Knapsack Problem - A Failing Greedy Algorithm

As stated, the knapsack problem has many variants. Instead of being able to take a fraction of items, in this version, we can either take the item or not. Revisiting our previous example, we have a 50 kg capacity knapsack and three items: 10 kg of gold valued at 60K, 20 kg of silver valued at 100K, and 30 kg of copper valued at 20K. If we follow the same logic as before, we would look at the price per kg and start filling the knapsack with gold (6K/kg), silver (5K/kg), and then copper (4K/kg) until we run out of space. In this situation, once we put gold and silver in the knapsack, we have 30 kg of material, so with only 20 kg of space left, we have to leave behind the copper. This gives us a total value of 160K. The problem is that even though the copper is less per kg, it has more overall value. In this example, leaving the gold allows us to take the silver and copper, at a total value of 220K. To efficiently solve this problem, we need to turn to dynamic programming.

9.3 Memoization vs Tabulation in Dynamic Programming

When approaching a dynamic programming problem, there are two major techniques: memoization and tabulation. Memoization is a top-down approach where we solve subproblems as they occur. This is typically done recursively with the results stored in a cache, usually a dictionary or list. This allows each subproblem to only be solved once. Tabulation is a bottom-up approach where the subproblems are solved in sequence before the main problem is approached. This avoids recursion but may lead to more subproblems being solved than are needed to solve the main problem.

Memoization is best for naturally recursive problems, especially if only a subset of results is required. Tabulation tends to work in situations where there is a large input or where memoization would lead to deep recursion. Tabulation tends to offer better performance overall.

To see the difference between these approaches, we can use a coin change problem as an example. Given a set of denominations and an amount of money, we look at the minimum number of each denomination to make that amount. To simplify our discussion, we will use coins.

A brute force approach would be to start with the total amount and see how we can break it down using each denomination. After every combination has been checked, we can return the level of recursion and the number of coins for each combination. The brute force recursive method would be intensive, as can be seen in Figure 9.4, for the simple task of determining the minimum possible change for 6 cents.

Figure 9.4   **Making change for 6 cents, using 1 and 5-cent coins**

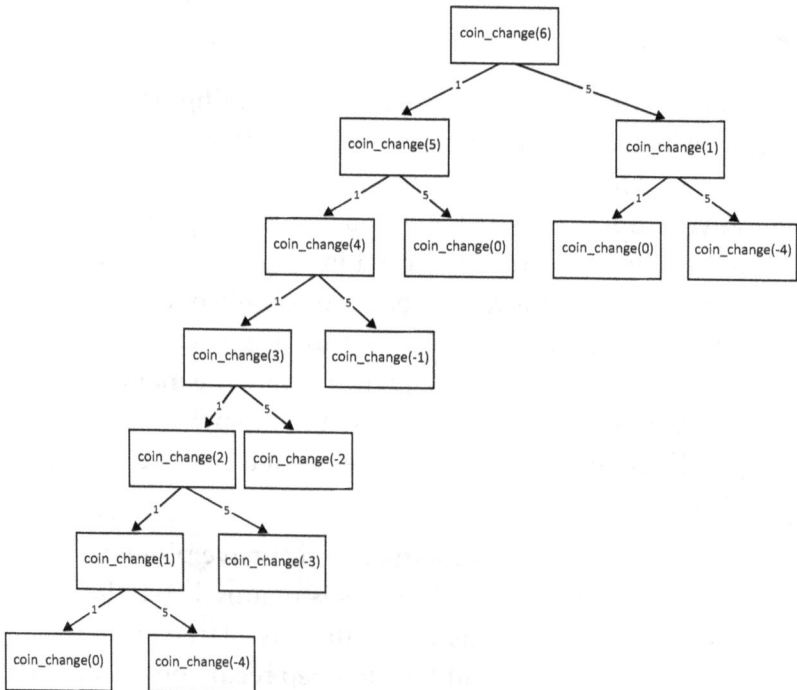

It should be evident that dynamic programming could be of use here, especially when dealing with higher values.

Memoization uses a top-down approach so that subproblems only need to be solved once. This version ensures the solution dictionary is created and then checks if the subproblem is already solved. As well, the base case and invalid cases where we go into negatives are checked and returned.

It's only after we get past these checks that we loop through our coins and recursively check the remainders after subtracting the current coin. Once a result is returned, we store it in our dictionary and return the minimum amount.

```python
def coin_change_memo(coins, amount, memo=None):
    #upfront checks
    if memo is None:
        memo = {}
    if amount in memo:
        return memo[amount]
    #base cases
    if amount == 0:
        return 0
    if amount < 0:
        return float('inf')

    min_coins = float('inf')
    for coin in coins:
        res = coin_change_memo(
            coins, amount - coin, memo
        )
```

```
if res != float('inf'):
   min_coins = min(min_coins, 1 + res)


memo[amount] = min_coins
return min_coins
```

This results in a time complexity that is based on the amount passed in and the number of coins being used, giving us $O(A \times n)$, where A is the amount and n is the number of coin denominations. The space complexity is based on the amount passed in. Since we are storing information for memoization, we have $O(A)$ space complexity as well as the $O(A)$ complexity for the recursion. Since both are linear, we can just call it $O(A)$ overall.

Compared to brute force, this is a huge improvement in time complexity. Due to the recursive nature, the complexity of brute force would be $O(n^A)$. The space complexity is $O(A)$ due to the recursion.

We can also approach this in a top-down approach using tabulation. When dealing with 1-cent coins, we end up storing information on every possible subproblem leading up to the current subproblem, so instead of waiting until we reach the subproblem to solve it, we can just solve all the subproblems first. This eliminates the need for recursion, cutting down on some of the space requirements.

Since we know we'll be storing all the subproblems, we can start all of them at infinity and set the value at index 0 to 0 coins. A list is perfect for these since the index will match up with the subproblem amount. We then start with each coin amount and see how many coins it takes to get to the target values, then move to the next coin type and update where there are improvements.

```python
def coin_change_memo(coins, amount, memo=None):
  #upfront checks
  if memo is None:
    memo = {}
  if amount in memo:
    return memo[amount]
  #base cases
  if amount == 0:
    return 0
  if amount < 0:
    return float('inf')

  min_coins = float('inf')
  for coin in coins:
    res = coin_change_memo(
      coins, amount - coin, memo
      )
    if res != float('inf'):
      min_coins = min(min_coins, 1 + res)

  memo[amount] = min_coins
  return min_coins

def coin_change_tab(coins, amount):
  dp = [float('inf')] * (amount + 1)
  dp[0] = 0

  for coin in coins:
    for i in range(coin, amount + 1):
      dp[i] = min(dp[i], dp[i - coin] + 1)
```

```
return (
    dp[amount] if dp[amount] != float('inf') else -1
)
```

This version has the same time complexity as the memoization version. The space complexity is still O(A) but avoids the recursion memory use, making this the optimal version for this problem.

9.4 Dynamic Programming Examples

9.4.1 0/1 Knapsack Problem

With the concept of DP in mind, we can re-examine our 0/1 knapsack problem. Using tabulation, we can solve smaller knapsacks with fewer items as our subproblems and work our way up to the final problem.

Our previous example used 10 kg of gold valued at 60K, 20 kg of silver valued at 100K, and 30 kg of copper valued at 20K, and a 50 kg capacity knapsack.

Let's start with a 10 kg capacity knapsack and only gold, followed by gold and silver, and finally with all three metals. We always start with the newest added metal and compare it with the previous subproblem. It is typical to store solutions in a table. Here, rows represent the number of items, and columns represent the capacity of the knapsacks. For each step, we decide if the new item fits or if it is worth taking.

	10 kg	Logic
Gold	60	Gold fits and has a value of 60
Gold and silver	60	Silver doesn't fit. We use the gold solution of 60, since it is better than 0.
Gold, silver, and copper	60	Copper doesn't fit. We use the gold and silver solution of 60, since it is better than 0.

We repeat for a 20 kg knapsack. The 20 kg knapsack will at least hold the same value as the 10 kg version.

	10 kg	20 kg	Logic
Gold	60	60	Gold fits and has a value of 60. There is no more to add.
Gold and silver	60	100	Silver fits with no more capacity. 100 is more than 60.
Gold, silver, and copper	60	100	Copper doesn't fit. We use the gold and silver solution of 100, since it is better than 0.

As we start having capacity left over, we look at the optimal solution for the capacity with 1 fewer metal.

	10 kg	20 kg	30 kg	Logic
Gold	60	60	60	Gold fits and has a value of 60. There is no more to add.
Gold and silver	60	100	160	Silver fits with 10 kg left. Add the value of silver to the gold solution of 10 kg. 160 is more than 60.
Gold, silver, and copper	60	100	160	Copper fits with no more capacity. We use the gold and silver solution of 160, since it is better than 120.

We continue this until we've built up the entire solution.

	10 kg	20 kg	30 kg	40 kg	Logic
Gold	60	60	60	60	Gold fits and has a value of 60. There is no more to add.
Gold and silver	60	100	160	160	Silver fits with 20 kg left. Add the value of silver to the gold solution of 20 kg. 160 is more than 60.
Gold, silver, and copper	60	100	160	180	Copper fits with 10 kg left. We add the value of copper to the gold and silver 10 kg solution, giving 180. We use 180 since it is better than 160.

	10 kg	20 kg	30 kg	40 kg	50 kg	Logic
Gold	60	60	60	60	60	Gold fits and has a value of 60. There is no more to add.
Gold and silver	60	100	160	160	160	Silver fits with 30 kg left. Add the value of silver to the gold solution of 30 kg. 160 is more than 60.
Gold, silver, and copper	60	100	160	180	220	Copper fits with 20 kg left. We add the value of copper to the gold and silver 20 kg solution, giving 220. We use 220 since it is better than 160.

The best combination gives a value of 220K. We can trace back through our table to determine which items were taken by seeing where the value changes occur. We look at the bottom right value of 220 and see if the value above is different. Since in this case it is, we know copper was taken, which uses up 30 kg of space. Now we look at the 20 kg subproblem for gold and silver, which has a value of 100K. Checking the above value, we can see that silver has indeed been taken. Since silver is 20 kg, we have no more capacity.

We could have stored the metals to solve each subproblem; however, this takes up more space, and the traceback is fairly simple.

In code, we start by building our table using a list of lists. Much like our example, we look at the items and decide if we can take the item. If so, we then decide whether we should take it based on the subproblem without the item at the same capacity.

```
def knapsack_dp(items, capacity):
  n = len(items)

  # Create a DP table initialized to 0
  dp = [
    [0] * (capacity + 1)
    for _ in range(n + 1)
  ]

  # Fill the table
  for i in range(1, n + 1):
    weight = items[i-1]['weight']
    value = items[i-1]['value']
    for w in range(1, capacity + 1):
      if weight > w:
        # Can't take the item
        dp[i][w] = dp[i-1][w]
```

```
        else:
            # Take or skip
            dp[i][w] = max(
                dp[i-1][w],
                value + dp[i-1][w - weight]
            )


    return dp
```

Likewise, for the traceback, we start at the bottom right of our table and determine if the item was taken based on the solution to the previous subproblem. If so, we append it to our solution list and subtract its weight from the capacity. Here we are reversing the order of the items so it reflects the way they were passed in.

```
def knapsack_traceback(dp, items, capacity):
    n = len(items)
    w = capacity
    selected_items = []

    for i in range(n, 0, -1):
        if dp[i][w] != dp[i-1][w]:
            # Item i-1 was taken
            selected_items.append(items[i-1]['name'])
            # Decrease the remaining weight
            w -= items[i-1]['weight']

    # Reverse to maintain original order
    return selected_items[::-1]
```

Here's the example we used; however, much larger lists can be easily handled by this method. The time complexity is based on both the number of items and the weight. Based on the two for loops, it should be no surprise that the time complexity is O(n x W). The space complexity is also O(n x W) based on the table created to hold the subproblem solutions.

```python
# Example usage
items = [
  {'name':'Gold', 'value':60, 'weight':10},
  {'name':'Silver', 'value':100, 'weight':20},
  {'name':'Gold', 'value':120, 'weight':30},
]

capacity = 50

#Build the DP table

dp_table = knapsack_dp(items, capacity)

# Total best value
best_value = dp_table[len(items)][capacity]
print(f"Best total value: {best_value}")

# Traceback to find which items were selected
selected = knapsack_traceback(
  dp_table, items, capacity
)
print("Selected items:", selected)
```

9.4.2 Rod Cutting Problem

Another common DP problem is rod cutting. The idea is that we have a rod of some length, which we can cut into any whole number of lengths to sell. Each length has its selling price, and we want to find the optimal price. While a different problem, there are some similarities to the knapsack problem, and the same logic can be applied. We can determine the best way to sell a 1-inch rod and then use this to help inform us for a 2-inch rod, until we reach our target length. Like most DP problems, it is great to start with a concrete example to work out by hand and then apply the logic to code.

To keep things simple, let's start with a 6-inch rod, which can be sold at the prices listed in Table 9.2.

Table 9.2 **Current rod prices**

Rod Length	Price
1	2
2	7
3	9
4	10
5	12
6	17

Quickly, we can see that a rod of length 0 is worth nothing, and a rod of length 1 is worth $2. When looking at longer lengths, we will look at how much we can cut off and look at the optimal value for the remainder.

For a rod of length 2, we have an optimal price of $7 when we sell a 2-inch section.

Cut Section	Price	Remainder	Optimal Price (looked up)	Total
2	7	0	0	7
1	2	1	2	4

For a rod of length 3, we have an optimal price of $9. While all three cuts produce the optimal value, we will record the smallest cut: 1. We can look at the solution for the remainder to see that it would be a 2-inch section, resulting in a 1-inch section and a 2-inch section.

Cut Section	Price	Remainder	Optimal Price (looked up)	Total
3	9	0	0	9
2	7	1	2	9
1	2	2	7	9

For a rod of length 4, we have an optimal price of $14 with a 2-inch cut.

Cut Section	Price	Remainder	Optimal Price (looked up)	Total
4	10	0	0	10
3	9	1	2	11
2	7	2	7	14
1	2	3	9	11

For a rod of length 5, we have an optimal price of $16 with a 3-inch cut.

Cut Section	Price	Remainder	Optimal Price (looked up)	Total
5	12	0	0	12
4	10	1	2	12
3	9	2	7	16
2	7	3	9	15
1	2	4	14	16

Finally, for a rod of length 6, we will get $21. This is with a 2-inch cut. Tracing back the solution for 4 inches, we find it is best to cut 2 inches, with the other 2 inches as another section. A rod of length 6 can be cut into three 2-inch sections for $21.

Cut Section	Price	Remainder	Optimal Price (looked up)	Total
6	17	0	0	17
5	12	1	2	14
4	10	2	7	17
3	9	3	9	18
2	7	4	14	21
1	2	5	16	18

Our code follows the same logic for constructing the DP table, although for readability, we start with a cut of 1 and work our way up to the full length. We only store the optimal result and the first cut made to obtain the result in separate lists.

```
def rod_cutting(prices, n):
    # dp[i] = max value for rod of length i
    dp = [0] * (n + 1)
    # first_cut[i] = first cut length leading to
    # best value
    first_cut = [0] * (n + 1)

    for length in range(1, n + 1):
        max_value = float('-inf')
        for cut_length in range(1, length + 1):
            if cut_length < len(prices):
                current_value = (
                    prices[cut_length]
                    + dp[length - cut_length]
                )
```

```
        if current_value > max_value:
          max_value = current_value
          first_cut[length] = cut_length
          # If tie: keep existing first_cut[length]
          # (smallest cut remains)
      dp[length] = max_value

    return dp, first_cut
```

To get the cuts to obtain the optimal result, we check our first cut list and move back by the amount of the cut. This gives us an efficient way to reconstruct the cuts required.

```
def reconstruct_cuts(first_cut, n):
  cuts = []
  while n > 0:
    cuts.append(first_cut[n])
    n -= first_cut[n]
  return cuts
```

To use this, we simply pass our information into the rod_cutting() function and then reconstruct the cuts. Since we have to build up the table by comparing the length to the number of cuts that can make up that length, we end up with $O(n^2)$ time complexity. Since we are storing the information in a one-dimensional list, we have a space complexity of $O(n)$.

```
prices = [0, 2, 7, 9, 10, 12, 17]
n = 6

dp, first_cut = rod_cutting(prices, n)
```

```
print(
    f"Maximum value for rod of length {n}: ${dp[n]}"
)

cuts = reconstruct_cuts(first_cut, n)
print(f"Cuts to make: {cuts}")
```

9.4.3 Longest Common Subsequence (LCS)

Another common DP problem is to find the longest subsequence that appears in two sequences. These sequences do not necessarily need to be continuous, but do have to be in the correct order. For example, considering the strings "WHALES" and "WHEELS", we have several subsequences, such as "WH", "WHES", and "WELS". Between these strings, the longest subsequence is 4.

A brute force solution to this would be to figure out all possible subsequences of "WHALES" and to loop through "WHEELS" to see if it contains the same substring. The time complexity here would be $O(m \times 2^n)$, where m is the length of the second string and n is the length of the first string. This is not acceptable.

Using dynamic programming, we can break this down into subproblems and solve them, reusing the solutions to help with the larger problems. Surprisingly, this problem shares a lot in common with the knapsack problem.

We can start by looking at shorter length strings. The table 9.3 has the first row populated by zeros representing comparing "W", "WH", "WHA", "WHAL", "WHALE","WHALES" against an empty string. The same logic holds for the first column, comparing the subsequences of an empty string to "W", "WH", "WHE", "WHEE", "WHEEL", and "WHEELS".

Table 9.3 **The start of a DP table for a subsequence problem**

		W	H	A	L	E	S
	0	0	0	0	0	0	0
W	0						
H	0						
E	0						
E	0						
L	0						
S	0						

The logic here is to check to see if a single character is in both strings, and then to add the results from the previous subproblems. For example, we check if the "W" in "WHALES" is common to the "W" in "WHEELS". Since there is a match, we add 1 to the previous subproblem, which can be found on the diagonal cell to the upper left. That is to say that the result of comparing "W" to "W" is 1 better than comparing "" to "".

Next, we compare the "H" to the "W". Not surprisingly, it is not a match. This time, look at the previous characters' subscores found above and to the left. Since comparing "H" to "" was 0 and "W" to "W" was 1, we record 1. What this means is that the largest subsequence between "WH" and "W" is 1 due to the match between the "W" and "W". We complete this row and the next with the same logic.

		W	H	A	L	E	S
	0	0	0	0	0	0	0
W	0	1	1	1	1	1	1
H	0	1	2	2	2	2	2
E	0	1	2	2	2	3	3
E	0						
L	0						
S	0						

The great thing about this process is that it allows us to accurately track the sequence of values without explicitly having to track what we have seen before. Looking up previous subproblem solutions helps us with that. Note that the second "E" in wheels didn't get counted twice, and that the "L" after the "E"s in "WHEELS" didn't increase the count since it is out of sequence.

		W	H	A	L	E	S
	0	0	0	0	0	0	0
W	0	1	1	1	1	1	1
H	0	1	2	2	2	2	2
E	0	1	2	2	2	3	3
E	0	1	2	2	2	3	3
L	0	1	2	2	3	3	3
S	0	1	2	2	3	3	4

We get a total solution of 4 by looking at the final cell in the table. To get the actual subsequence, we can trace back through the table starting at the last cell. This is a little different than the knapsack problem as we are checking whether the two characters are equal at that location. If so, we know that character is part of the sequence, and we move diagonally. If not, we either move left or up, choosing

the path through Bob (3+1 = 4) and the path through David (2+1=3) and see which is greatest. Alice's maximum length is 4. Table 9.4 shows our completed results.

Table 9.4   Maximum length of influence chain

Alice	4
Bob	3
Charlie	2
David	2
Eve	1

We continue through the other nodes, quickly looking up the values we already calculated.

In code, we follow a typical DFS, but store the final values in the memoization list, significantly reducing redundancy.

```
def dfs_longest_chain_dp(graph, node, memo):
    if node in memo:
        return memo[node]

    max_length = 0
    for neighbor, _ in graph.get_neighbors(node):
        length = dfs_longest_chain_dp(
            graph, neighbor, memo
        )
        max_length = max(max_length, length)

    memo[node] = 1 + max_length
    return memo[node]
```

The main function is nearly identical to our graph example, minus the visited set.

```
def find_longest_influence_chain_dp(graph):
   longest_user = None
   longest_chain = 0
   memo = {}

   for user in graph.adj_list:
     chain_length = dfs_longest_chain_dp(
       graph, user, memo
       )
     if chain_length > longest_chain:
       longest_chain = chain_length
       longest_user = user

   return longest_user, longest_chain
```

Since we have removed the recomputation of nodes, we only need to visit every node and edge once. This reduces our time complexity down to O(V + E), which is much more reasonable than our O(V x (V+E)) from before. Our space complexity is O(V) due to the memoization and the recursion depth.

Chapter Summary

- Dynamic programming solves problems by solving overlapping subproblems.

- Storing the results of subproblems avoids repeated work.

- Memoization uses a top-down approach while tabulation uses a bottom-up approach.

- Choosing between greedy strategies and dynamic programming depends on understanding the problem and determining if optimal substructure and overlapping subproblems exist.

Quiz

1. **Which best describes dynamic programming?**
   a. Only solving the largest possible problems
   b. Storing results of subproblems to avoid recomputation
   c. Using random choices to find approximate solutions
   d. Using recursion as the underlying method

2. **What property must a problem have for dynamic programming to work correctly?**
   a. A small number of states
   b. The greedy-choice property
   c. Overlapping subproblems
   d. Randomized structure

3. **Which describes tabulation?**
   a. Bottom-up
   b. Middle-out
   c. Top-down
   d. Randomized

4. **What happens if a greedy algorithm is applied to a problem without the greedy-choice property?**
   a. It may find a less-than-optimal solution
   b. It still guarantees the optimal solution
   c. It will find multiple solutions
   d. It will not find a solution

Case Studies and Real-World Problems

Case Study 1: Managing a Music Library

When tackling real-world programming problems, it is important to remember that there is rarely a single "best" solution. Different programmers may choose different strategies based on their experience and priorities. Problem-solving in programming can be a creative process as well as a technical one.

In this case study, we are tasked with creating a music management system. The system should be able to store songs, allow searching, and enable users to build playlists. The system should be able to handle thousands of songs.

As an exercise, you should attempt this case study on your own before reading the potential solution. The potential solution, along with some hints, follows the detailed constraints and task.

Constraints

- Searches should remain reasonably fast as the number of songs grows.
- Some song fields may be missing.
- Searches should not be case-sensitive.
- Sorting should be available by title or duration.
- Playlists should allow easy adding and removing of songs.

Task

Build the main structure for a music library. Ensure:

- An appropriate data structure is used to allow easy storage and searching of songs.
- Songs can be searched by title, artist, or album.
- Adding and removing songs is implemented.
- An appropriate sorting algorithm is used.
- Time and space complexity are considered.

Hints

- A list can be used for the ordered storage of all songs and playlists.
- Hash tables can be used for fast lookups.
- The String method `lower()` can be used to normalize text.
- Insertion sort is efficient when dealing with nearly sorted lists.
- Binary search is efficient for large, ordered lists.

...le Solution

We'll start by creating a song class that will store the title, artist, and album. Since we could have incomplete entries, we will use the default values of None for the artist and album. We can overwrite the __str__ method to provide a readable string to display the song information when printed.

```
class Song:
    def __init__(
        self, title, artist=None, album=None
    ):
        self.title = title
        self.artist = artist
        self.album = album

    def __str__(self):
        return (
            f"{self.title}- {self.artist}-"
            f"{self.album}"
        )
```

We use a modified version of insertion sort to organize our song list by title as new songs are added. To remove case sensitivity, we use the lower() method to normalize the strings. Normally, it would be more efficient to use other sorting methods, but since our list is sorted each time we add a new song, ours is the best-case scenario.

```
def insertion_sort(array):
    for i in range(1, len(array)):
        value = array[i]
        j = i - 1
        while (
            j >= 0
            and array[j].title.lower()
                > value.title.lower()
        ):
            array[j + 1] = array[j]
            j -= 1
        array[j + 1] = value
```

While we could use Python dictionaries, we will use our HashTable class, modified slightly to normalize the strings.

```
class HashTable:
    def __init__(self, size=1000):
        self.size = size
        self.table = [[] for _ in range(self.size)]

    def _hash(self, key):
        return hash(key.lower()) % self.size

    def insert(self, key, value):
        index = self._hash(key)
        self.table[index].append((key, value))

    def get(self, key):
        index = self._hash(key)
        return [
            v for k, v in self.table[index]
            if k.lower() == key.lower()
        ]
```

The `view_playlist` method simply returns the list of songs if the playlist exists or an empty list if it doesn't.

```
def create_playlist(self, name, song_titles):
    playlist = []
    for title in song_titles:
      match = self.search_by_title(title)
      if match:
        playlist.append(match)
    self.playlists[name] = playlist

    def view_playlist(self, name):
      return self.playlists.get(name, [])
```

By thinking about data structures and algorithm design, we can create programs that run efficiently. Table 10.1 shows the comparison of the time complexity of our approach and a typical unoptimized approach. Note that the space complexities of both are roughly comparable.

Table 1   **Comparing complexity where n is the number of songs, and m is the number of songs to add to a playlist**

Operation	Optimized Time Complexity	Unoptimized Time Complexity
Adding song	O(n)	O(n log n)
Searching by Title	O(log n)	O(n)
Searching by Artist or Album	O(1)	O(n)
Creating Playlist	O(m log n)	O(m n)
Viewing Playlist	O(1)	O(1)

Through this case study, we gain practical experience in applying core programming concepts. Thoughtful choices in data structures and algorithms can significantly improve the performance and scalability of the programs we build. By focusing on optimization and efficient design, we continue to grow as more skilled and confident programmers.

Further Resources

Two bonus case studies are available online:

- *Case Study 2 — Managing Customer Support Resources*

- *Case Study 3 — Warehouse Organization and Efficient Product Placement*

How to access

1. Go to the book's product page at
   www.vibrantpublishers.com

2. Click **Request Sample Book/Online Resource**

3. Choose **Online Resource**, select **user type**, submit

4. Check your email
   —or simply scan the QR code.

Bibliography

1. A. Padma Reddy, Data Structures and Algorithms Using C++ (Chennai: SciTech Publications, 2009), 5–8.

2. Brad Miller and David Ranum. Problem *Solving with Algorithms and Data Structures Using Python.* 3rd ed.

3. GeeksforGeeks. "GeeksforGeeks | Your All-in-One Learning Portal." https://www.geeksforgeeks.org.

4. geopy 2.4.1 Documentation. Accessed April 6, 2025. https://geopy.readthedocs.io/en/stable/#

5. Krišjānis Kazaks. "Rows of black chairs". May 11, 2022. Unsplash. https://unsplash.com/photos/rows-of-black-chairs-BH3C4ClT0PY

6. LeetCode. "LeetCode – The World's Leading Online Programming Learning Platform." https://leetcode.com.

7. Nadjib BR. "Brown and beige ceiling lamp". December 25, 2020. Unsplash. https://unsplash.com/photos/brown-and-beige-ceiling-lamp-51Ms-0PbCHo

8. Python Software Foundation. "collections — Container Datatypes." Python 3.12 Documentation. Accessed December 1, 2024. https://docs.python.org/3/library/collections.html.

9. Python Software Foundation. "Data Model." Python 3 Documentation. Accessed December 13, 2024. https://docs.python.org/3/reference/datamodel.html#object.__hash__.

10. Python Software Foundation. "Time Complexity in Python." Accessed November 28, 2024. https://wiki.python.org/moin/TimeComplexity.

11. Python Software Foundation. The array module — Python 3.12.0 documentation. Accessed November 28, 2024. https://docs.python.org/3/library/array.html.

12. Sanjoy Dasgupta, Christos Papadimitriou, and Umesh Vazirani. *Algorithms.* New York: McGraw-Hill, 2006.

13. SEON. Global Banking Fraud Index 2023. Accessed October 18, 2024. https://seon.io/resources/global-banking-fraud-index-2023/.

14. SimpleMaps. U.S. Cities Database. Accessed April 6, 2025. https://simplemaps.com/data/us-cities.

15. Thomas H. Cormen, Charles E. Leiserson, Ronald L. Rivest, and Clifford Stein, Introduction to Algorithms, 4th ed. (Cambridge, MA: MIT Press, 2022), 9.

16. Torbjørn Helgesen. "A pen sitting on top of a piece of paper". June 9, 2021. Unsplash. https://unsplash.com/photos/a-green-pen-sitting-on-top-of-a-piece-of-paper-KXfiLw0HrvU

Glossary

Abstract Data Type (ADT): A data model defined by its behavior rather than its implementation.

Adjacency List: A graph representation where each vertex has a list of its neighboring vertices, often with edge weights.

Adjacency Matrix: A graph representation where a 2D array stores information about connections between all pairs of vertices.

Algorithm: A step-by-step procedure designed to solve a specific problem or accomplish a defined task.

Array: A collection of elements of the same data type in a continuous block of memory.

Big O Notation: A notation used to describe the upper bound of an algorithm's time or space complexity, expressing how it scales with input size.

Binary Search: An efficient search algorithm for finding an item from a sorted list of items by repeatedly dividing the search interval in half.

Binary Search Tree (BST): A special type of binary tree where nodes are arranged so the values in the left subtree are less than the parent, and the values in the right subtree are greater.

Binary Tree: A hierarchical data structure where each node has at most two children.

Breadth-First Search (BFS): A traversal algorithm that explores all nodes at the current level before moving to nodes at the next level.

Brute Force Algorithm: A straightforward, but typically inefficient, method of solving a problem by trying all possible solutions until the correct one is forward.

Chaining: A collision resolution technique in hash tables where a linked list is used to store values that hash to the same index.

Collision: Occurs in a hash table when two different keys hash to the same index.

Data Structure: A method of organizing and storing data so that it can be accessed and modified efficiently.

Depth: The number of edges from the root node to a specific node in a tree.

Depth-First Search (DFS): A graph traversal algorithm that explores as far as possible along a path before backtracking using a stack or recursion.

Dijkstra's Algorithm: An algorithm used to find the shortest paths between nodes in a graph with non-negative edge weights.

Directed Graph: A graph where edges have a specific direction.

Divide-and-conquer: An algorithmic strategy that involves breaking a problem into smaller subproblems.

Dynamic Programming (DP): An algorithmic technique for solving complex problems by breaking them down into simple, overlapping subproblems and storing the results to avoid recomputation.

Edge: A connection between two vertices in a graph.

Floyd-Warshall Algorithm: An algorithm for finding the shortest paths in a weighted graph that computes the shortest paths between pairs of vertices.

Flowchart: A visual representation of the steps in an algorithm or process.

FIFO (First In, First Out): Used in queues, the first element added is the first to be removed for processing.

Fractional Knapsack Problem: A variant of the knapsack problem where fractions of items can be taken.

Greedy Algorithm: An algorithm that makes the locally optimal choice at each step with the hope of finding the global optimum.

Hash function: A function that takes an input, or key, and returns a numerical value to determine the key's index in a hash table.

Hash table: A data structure that maps keys to values using a hash function, allowing for efficient data retrieval.

Height: The number of edges on the longest path from the root node to a leaf node in a tree.

Iteration: The repetition of a set of operations in a loop until a condition is met.

Iterative: An approach to problem-solving that uses loops to repeat a block of code until a condition is met.

Leaf node: A node in a tree with no children.

LIFO (Last In, First Out): Used in stacks, the last element added is the first to be removed for processing.

Linked List: A linear data structure in which elements (nodes) are stored in non-contiguous memory locations. Each node points to the next one.

Load factor: In a hash table, the ratio of stored values to the number of bins in the table.

Longest common subsequence (LCS): A dynamic programming problem that involves finding the longest subsequence common to two sequences. The subsequence does not need to be contiguous.

Memoization: A technique used in dynamic programming where previously computed results are stored to avoid redundant calculations.

Merge sort: A divide-and-conquer sorting algorithm that recursively splits an array into halves, sorts them, and then merges the sorted halves.

Modular Design: A design principle where a problem is divided into separate, independent parts that can be developed, tested, and reused independently.

Modulo Hashing: A simple hash function that involves taking the key and getting the modulo of it with the size of the hash table to determine the bin.

Nodes: The fundamental units of trees and graphs. Often called vertices in graphs.

O(1) complexity: Constant. The time or memory remains constant regardless of the size of the data.

O(n) complexity: Linear. The time or memory use grows linearly with the size of the input.

O(n²) complexity: Quadratic. The time or memory use grows proportional to the squared size of the input.

O(2ⁿ) complexity: Exponential. The time or memory use doubles with each additional input element. This leads to extremely rapid growth and becomes impractical even for small input sizes.

O(n log n) complexity: Log-linear. The time or memory use grows slightly faster than linear but much slower than quadratic. It scales with the size of the input multiplied by its logarithm.

O(log n) complexity: Logarithmic. The time or memory use grows logarithmically. Optimal for larger inputs.

Optimal substructure: A property of a problem where an optimal solution can be constructed from the optimal solutions of its subproblems, making it suitable for dynamic programming.

Overlapping subproblems: A property of a problem where the same subproblems are solved multiple times, making it suitable for dynamic programming.

Pivot: An element chosen in the quicksort algorithm around which the array is partitioned. Elements smaller are moved before, and those larger are moved after.

Pointers: Variables that store memory address where data is located, rather than the data itself.

Push: An operation that adds an element to the top of a stack.

Pop: An operation that removes and returns the top element from a stack.

Pseudocode: A simplified, language-independent way of describing the steps in an algorithm.

Queue: A linear data structure that follows the FIFO (First In, First Out) principle.

Quicksort: A highly efficient, in-place sorting algorithm that uses a divide-and-conquer strategy, partitioning around a pivot element.

Recursion: A method in which a function calls itself to solve a problem by breaking it down into smaller instances of the same problem.

Scalability: The ability of an algorithm or system to handle a growing amount of work or input data efficiently.

Set: An unordered collection of unique elements.

Space complexity: A measure of how the memory usage of an algorithm increases as the size of the input increases.

Stack: A linear data structure that follows the LIFO (Last In, First Out) principle.

Tabulation: A dynamic programming technique that builds solutions to subproblems from the bottom-up, usually iteratively filling a table.

Theta Notation: A tight bound analysis, describing the average-case performance of an algorithm.

Time complexity: A measure of how the run time of an algorithm increases as the size of the input increases.

Trie (Prefix Tree): A tree data structure used to store strings, where nodes represent common prefixes. Useful for autocomplete and spell checking.

Undirected Graph: A graph where edges have no direction. The connections automatically go both ways.

Unweighted Graph: A graph where edges do not have weights, meaning all connections are equal.

Vertex: A fundamental unit of a graph, also known as a node.

Weighted Graph: A graph where edges have weights, representing costs, distances, or other measures.

0/1 Knapsack Problem: A variant of the knapsack problem where only whole items can be taken.